Fresl

O

Dr SIEGLINDE McGEE

Set in 10 pt Garamond

ISBN 978-1-0913444-1-9

Cover: High-class sprinter Hot Streak who stands at
Tweenhills Farm & Stud. Photo by Sieglinde McGee

Disclaimer

Every effort has been made to ensure that the information in
this book is accurate and up to date. The author accepts no
liability or responsibility for any loss or damage caused, or
thought to be caused, by anything contained within the book.

ABOUT THE AUTHOR

Sieglinde discovered horse racing by chance on Grand National day 1982 and was instantly hooked, reading and watching everything she could about it. She started writing on the subject in the summer of 1983, began keeping personal databases on racing and pedigrees the following year, and got her first job in racing five years after that – doing course wires (tipping) and bloodstock sales reports for *The Sporting Life*, maintaining a small pedigree database, and producing press releases for a major stud.

She has been widely published on racing and pedigrees over the past three decades, wrote and produced her own non-published 'Timeform Annual-style' books for several years in the 1990s, has been writing for *The Irish Field* since the spring of 2000, and on her own website (www.sieglindemcgee.com) for the past three years.

In 2005, she was conferred with a doctorate from Trinity College Dublin for a thesis titled *Behavioural Reactivity and Ensuing Temperamental Traits in Young Thoroughbred Racehorses (Equus caballus)* – the culmination of four years of postgraduate research. She is also a graduate of Dublin City University and of the world-famous Thoroughbred Breeding course at the Irish National Stud, and she taught in Trinity College Dublin and for Oscail (now DCU Connected) for several years.

ALSO BY THE AUTHOR

Racing / pedigrees:
European Group 1 Winners of 2018. Independently published, 2018. 396 pages. Paperback & ebook

New Sires of 2019. Independently published. 2019. 230 pages. Paperback & ebook.

Other:
Key Research & Study Skills in Psychology. SAGE, London, 2010. 210 pages. Hardback, paperback & ebook

INTRODUCTION

Offspring by freshman stallions provide added interest in two-year-old races throughout the season. Who among them may be a leading sire of the future? Are there any potential classic sires among them? Is the next Sadler's Wells, Galileo, Pivotal or Dubawi in their midst? Whose his first yearlings were too expensive? Who among these young horses may yield substantial returns with his latest yearling crop over what they cost as foals?

The stallion whose first two-year-old crop accumulates the highest earnings total is the one who is crowned Champion Freshman Sire, and it is hoped that most of that prize money came from stakes and pattern races and not the well-endowed sales races that distort the rankings. That said, quite often the horse who tops this table will eventually be overtaken by one or more of those who finished further down in the freshman rankings, so one should not lose heart if their stallion, favourite, or supported choice fails to win medals in that first year.

Large numbers of winners and races won may sound impressive, but which is better in the long run? Is it a stallion who produces stock of high quality, getting stakes and pattern winners and high-class handicappers, or one who notches up an eye-catching tally of claimers and platers, low-grade maiden winners and nursery horses from the scatter-gun approach of having large numbers of runners? The answer depends on what you're looking for in a stallion.

There are 44 members of the freshman class of 2019 reviewed here all of who stood in either Ireland, the United Kingdom, France, Germany, or the United States of America in 2016 and who had at least two yearlings sold in Europe. They include 24 individual Group/Grade 1 winners, a US Triple Crown hero, classic stars, top sprinters and milers, and leading two-year-olds. They also include National Hunt stallions, some horses who had a small first crop, one who is already dead, one who got a Group 1 winner in the Australian half of his global first crop hours before this book went to print, some no longer easily available, one who was withdrawn from service in his first year, gelded and returned to training, and one who is arguably one of the most exciting stallion prospects to go to stud since Sea The Stars and Frankel.

The pedigree and racing records of each are discussed, along with their prospects. The auction results for their first crop of yearlings are also included, organised by currency and also listing those who failed to sell (including vendor buy-backs). The latter are sorted in alphabetical order of their dams. Names of those sales horses are included where known at the time of going to print, and space is provided for the reader to add in further details if they wish. Almost all of the stallions will have offspring who were not consigned to the sales, many of whom will likely race for their breeders.

As with all of the books in this series, there are also many indexes in which the reviewed horses are organised. In this volume, these are: by the stud where they stood in 2016, their fee that year, by their sire, grandsire, great-grandsire, broodmare sire, date of their earliest win, the highest grade in which they won, the distances over which they won group races, the ages at which they achieved those feats, the going on which they got those wins, and by their current fee.

Where the are other stallions by the sire of the horse being reviewed, a selection of these is listed in his summary details section. The (Gr1) or similar notation shown by their name represents the highest level at which they have, so far, had at least one winner. If their eldest offspring are two-year-olds or will be yearlings or foals by the time of the northern hemisphere's autumn sales, then that is indicated instead.

Readers may notice that some horses have not been given a suffix with their names, in pedigree charts or the various indexes. This is not an error or an omission. The suffix indicates the country in which the horse was born, but those who were born in Ireland or Great Britain did not get suffixes until 1988. Therefore, horses born in those countries before that year do not have one.

Dr Sieglinde McGee
23rd March 2019

CONTENTS

AMARILLO (IRE)

Haras du Thenney's Amarillo was a triple pattern winner from six to seven furlongs – crowned champion older sprinter in Germany in 2014 – and notched up his easiest success when taking a mile listed contest by seven lengths on soft ground at Dusseldorf. His string of pattern placings feature a second to Amaron in the Group 1 Premio Vittorio di Capua, also over a mile, and although racing in a country not noted for its juvenile programme, he was a pattern-placed winner at two, the blacktype performance also coming over a mile.

He is an early stallion son for Holy Roman Emperor (by Danehill), a stallion whose 13 top-level winners include 2018 classic scorers Romanised and Well Timed, and he is out of Alte Kunst (by Royal Academy) who earned her blacktype when third in a mile listed contest. He is a half-brother to Art Antique (by Darshaan), who was pattern-placed over 10 furlongs, a slightly closer relation to mile Group 3 scorer Aslana (by Rock Of Gibraltar), and a grandson of the dual German champion Alte Zeit (by Surumu). She won both the Group 2 Preis der Diana (German Oaks) and Group 2 Schwarzgold-Rennen (German 1000 Guineas) and was runner-up to Luigi in the Group 1 Deutsches Derby.

With all of this on his page, Amarillo looks a likely candidate to produce some autumn and winter two-year-old winners and to have his best representatives in the broad six-to-12-furlong range at age three and upwards. There are 19 registered members of his first crop.

SUMMARY DETAILS

Stood in 2016: Haras du Thenney, France
Fee in 2016: €3,000
Career highlights: 6 wins inc John of Gaunt Stakes (Gr3), Flieger Preis (Gr3), Silberne Peitsche (Gr3), Bayerischer Fliegerpreis (L), Preis der Dreijahrigen (L), 2nd Premio Vittorio di Capua (Gr1), Challenge Stakes (Gr2), Mehl-Mulhens Rennen (Gr2), Prix de la Porte Maillot (Gr3), Grosser Preis der CGH Versicherungen (Gr3), Preis der Winterfavoriten (Gr3), Sparkasse Holstein Cup Flieger Preis (Gr3), Herbst Preis (L), 3rd Meilen Trophy (Gr2), Oppenheim-Rennen (L)

Standing in 2019: Gestut Helenenhof, Germany
Fee in 2019: €3,000
Stallions by his sire include: Leitir Mor (winners), Amarillo
(2yo), Mongolian Khan (2yo), Honorius (yearlings), Morandi
(yearlings)

AMARILLO (IRE) – bay 2009

Holy Roman Emperor (IRE)	Danehill (USA)	Danzig (USA)
		Razyana (USA)
	L'On Vite (USA)	Secretariat (USA)
		Fanfreluche (CAN)
Alte Kunst (IRE)	Royal Academy (USA)	Nijinsky (CAN)
		Crimson Saint (USA)
	Alte Zeit (GER)	Surumu (GER)
		Alte Welt (GER)

SALES YEARLINGS OF 2018

Sold in Euros

	bc - Final Whistle (by Rossini) - Osarus - September - €8,000
	bf - Olonella (by Selkirk) - Arqana - October - €8,000
Texas Girl (FR)	bf - Roxanna (by Myboycharlie) - BBAG - October - €7,500
Texas Girl (FR)	bf - Roxanna (by Myboycharlie) - Arqana - February - €4,000
Glorious Glorious (FR)	brf - La Beaute (by Ali-Royal) - BBAG - October - €2,500
Make Me Glorious (FR)	bc - Royale Requete (by Urgent Request) - BBAG - October - €1,500

Not Sold (inc. vendor buy-backs)

Moko (FR)	bf - Allez Hongkong (by Sakhee) - Arqana - November
Bella Amarilla (FR)	bf - Belle Et Royale (by Astronomer Royal) - Osarus - September
San Remo (GER)	bc - Saving Grace (by Manduro) - Baden-Baden - August

AMARILLO (IRE)

AMARON (GB)

A prolific pattern winner from seven to nine furlongs, Amaron's finest hour came when he beat Amarillo by a length in the Group 1 Premio Vittorio di Capua over a mile at San Siro. He also came within a nose of being classic-placed in France. In what was a blanket finish for the 2012 Group 1 Poule d'Essai des Poulains (French 2000 Guineas), Lucayan won by a short-neck from Veneto, with ill-fated Furner's Green the same margin back in third, a nose ahead of Amaron. There were additional short-necks back to the fifth and sixth, Gregorian and Dabirsim.

He is a son of leading international sire Shamardal (by Giant's Causeway), whose early stallion sons feature the top-class racehorse and sire Lope De Vega, and he is out of Amandalini (by Bertolini), an unraced half-sister to Grade 1-placed US 12-furlong Grade 2 scorer Persianlux (by Persian Bold). Third dam Tropicaro (by Caro) won the Group 1 Prix Marcel Boussac and took the runners-up spot in the Group 1 Prix Saint-Alary, her blacktype descendants include some talented middle-distance performers and stayers, and her siblings include Now That's Funny (by Saratoga Six) – the dam of Group 3 Jersey Stakes winner and Group 1 July Cup runner-up Lucayan Prince (by Fast Play).

Amaron stands at Gestut Etzean in Germany, and although he can be expected to get some two-year-old winners, it is likely to be as three-year-olds and older horses that his progeny show what they can do, with their best results coming in the broad six-to-14-furlong range. His initial yearlings met with mixed success in the auction ring, and his top-priced two, both fillies, achieved substantially higher prices than the rest of his representatives.

SUMMARY DETAILS

Stood in 2016: Gestut Etzean, Germany
Fee in 2016: €4,500
Career highlights: 9 wins inc Premio Vittorio di Capua (Gr1), Badener Meile (Gr2), Grosser Preis der Dortmunder Wirtschaft (Gr3), Fruhjahrs-Meile (Gr3-twice), Dr Busch Memorial (Gr3), Prix Perth (Gr3), Zukunfts Rennen (Gr3), Oppenheim-Rennen

(L), 2nd Oettingen Rennen (Gr2), 3rd Meilen Trophy (Gr2), Prix
Edmond Blanc (Gr3), Preis der Winterfavoriten (Gr3)
Standing in 2019: Gestut Etzean, Germany
Fee in 2019: €4,500
Stallions by his sire include: Captain Sonador (Gr1), Lope De
Vega (Gr1), Casamento (Gr2), Mukhadram (Gr3), Shamoline
Warrior (L), Ghibellines (winners), Gingerbread Man (winners),
Shakespearean (winners), Sommerabend (winners), Amaron (2yo),
Crackerjack King (2yo), French Navy (2yo), Zazou (2yo), Bow
Creek (yearlings), Dariyan (yearlings), Lightning Moon (yearlings),
Balios (foals), Doha Dream (new)

AMARON (GB) – chestnut 2009

Shamardal (USA)	Giant's Causeway (USA)	Storm Cat (USA)
		Mariah's Storm (USA)
	Helsinki (GB)	Machiavellian (USA)
		Helen Street
Amandalini (IRE)	Bertolini (USA)	Danzig (USA)
		Aquilegia (USA)
	Luxurious (USA)	Lyphard (USA)
		Tropicaro (FR)

SALES YEARLINGS OF 2018
Sold in Euros

	chf - Rondinay (by Cadeaux Genereux) - Baden-Baden - August - €160,000
Midnight (GER)	chf - Ma Coeur (by Sholokhov) - Baden-Baden - August - €75,000
Ancona (IRE)	chf - Amazone (by Adlerflug) - Baden-Baden - August - €20,000
Classic Mind (GER)	chc - Classic Diva (by Sholokhov) - Baden-Baden - August - €20,000
Royal Dancer (GER)	chc - Royal Princess (by Lord Of England) - Baden-Baden - August - €15,000
Dominator (GER)	chc - Dominate (by Monsun) - BBAG - October - €14,000
Tiramisu (GER)	bf - Tiger Lilly (by Tiger Hill) - BBAG - October - €8,500
Kryptic Key (GER)	chf - Key To Win (by Halling) - BBAG - October - €7,000

Turn Me On (GER)	bc - Tintagel (by Oasis Dream) - BBAG - October - €5,500
New Topmodel (GER)	bf - Napata (by Singspiel) - BBAG - October - €5,000
Waldzeit (GER)	chf - Wildente (by Linngari) - BBAG - October - €5,000
Nonplusultra (GER)	chf - Nocturna (by Dai Jin) - BBAG - October - €4,000
	bf - Rumina (by Dashing Blade) - BBAG - October - €3,000
Born To Race (GER)	chc - Bartlett Ruby (by Lord Of England) - BBAG - October - €2,000
	bc - Wonderful Time (by Next Desert) - BBAG - October - €2,000

Not Sold (inc. vendor buy-backs)

Ambrosius (GER)	bc - Albara (by Barathea) - BBAG - October
Bella Maron (GER)	bf - Bella Amica (by Black Sam Bellamy) - Baden-Baden - August
Candy Sweet (GER)	chf - Chalkidikis Elpida (by Mamool) - BBAG - October
Fabula (GER)	brf - Fortezza (by Law Society) - Baden-Baden - August
Hamaron (GER)	chc - Hungry Heidi (by Kheleyf) - BBAG - October
	bf - Ishika (by Lagunas) - BBAG - October
Kraichthaler (GER)	chc - Kellemoi De Papita (by Hawk Wing) - BBAG - October
Palmita (GER)	chf - Peace Flower (by Dashing Blade) - Baden-Baden - August
Palimero (GER)	bc - Pearl Of Love (by Sholokhov) - BBAG - October
Patchouli (GER)	grf - Pearl Royale (by Sholokhov) - BBAG - October

AMARON (GB)

AMERICAN PHAROAH (USA)

Many tried, some got close, but since Affirmed wrote his name into the record books in 1978, no horse swept the US Triple Crown until 2015. Some expressed doubt that the feat would ever be achieved again, but the current decade has seen two Triple Crown heroes: Justify in 2018 and American Pharoah three years before.

The Bob Baffert-trained son of Pioneerof The Nile (by Empire Maker) won nine of his 11 career starts, and aside from a fifth-place finish over six and a half furlongs at Del Mar on his debut in August of his two-year-old season, his only defeat was that shock three-quarter-length loss to Keen Ice in the Grade 1 Travers Stakes on his penultimate run. His aggregate winning margin was 44.5 lengths, and his widest margin of victory was eight lengths in the Arkansas Derby at Oaklawn Park, closely followed by his seven-length romp in the Preakness Stakes at Pimlico and his six-and-a-half-length career finale in the Breeders' Cup Classic at Keeneland.

Timeform rated him 126 at two and a massive 138 at three, placing him close to the all-time greats. Had there been anything around to give him a serious challenge at his peak, it's possible he could have achieved an even higher figure. His good looks and outstanding race record ensured that he would receive the best of support at stud, and that has translated into impressive results in the auction ring. Most exciting young stallions can boast of a handful or string of six-figure lots among their initial auction yearlings, but for American Pharoah, the handful was the few who failed to sell for at least that much. All but four of his large number of yearlings to sell fetched at least $100,000, with a string of them hitting at least $500,000 and five reaching seven figures.

His pedigree does not shout top stallion prospect, but the support he has attracted, how his early offspring have been received, and the initial reports that have been emerging on how they're training all combine to make him an exciting prospect. It will be quite a disappointment if he fails to become a leading sire.

He is one of three top-level winners among 23 blacktype scorers for his sire, and as a great-grandson of the classic star and notable sire Unbridled (by Fappiano), he represents a branch of

8

the Mr Prospector (by Raise a Native) sire line. Sadly, Pioneerof The Nile died suddenly just before this book went to print. He was only 13 years old.

American Pharoah's unraced dam Littleprincessemma (by Yankee Gentleman) is by a Storm Cat (by Storm Bird) horse who has got one Grade 1 winner among 21 blacktype scorers, and she is out of Exclusive Rosette (by Ecliptical), a listed-race winner in Florida by a minor sire son of Exclusive Native (by Raise A Native). His full-sister American Cleopatra was a runner-up in the Grade 1 Del Mar Debutante Stakes at two, his full-brother St Patrick's Day has been Group 3-placed in Ireland, and they have a two-year-old full-brother named Theprinceofthebes. Their half-sister Chasing Yesterday (by Tapit), on the other hand, was among the best members of a strong-looking US juvenile filly crop in 2018, winning three of her four starts including a seven-furlong listed contest at Del Mar in November, a month before a narrow success in the Grade 1 Starlet Stakes over eight and a half furlongs at Los Alamitos. That Bob Baffert-trained chestnut could be anything.

Littleprincessemma also has a couple of notable siblings – the speedy pair Storm Wolf (by Stormin Fever) and Misty Rosette (by Stormin Fever). The first-named won a Grade 2 contest over seven furlongs, his sister picked up a Grade 3 sprint and earned third place in the Grade 1 Test Stakes, and like their now famous sister, they are by a son of Storm Cat.

American Pharoah was a racehorse of rare brilliance and a top-class autumn two-year-old who became a superstar at three, and he has deservedly been given every opportunity to make an impact at stud. His best winners are likely to come in the broad six-to-12-furlong range, and if he fulfils his potential, then those will include leading juveniles, classic horses, and an array of stakes and graded winners as three-year-olds and older horses. It can be expected that he will have quite a few runners in Europe too, and it will be fascinating to see how his progeny fare under our racing conditions.

SUMMARY DETAILS

Stood in 2016: Ashford Stud, Kentucky
Fee in 2016: $200,000

Career highlights: 9 wins inc Breeders' Cup Classic (Gr1), Kentucky Derby (Gr1), Preakness Stakes (Gr1), Belmont Stakes (Gr1), Haskell Invitational Stakes (Gr1), Arkansas Derby (Gr1), Del Mar Futurity (Gr1), Forerunner Stakes (Gr1), Rebel Stakes (Gr2), 2nd Travers Stakes (Gr1)
Standing in 2019: Ashford Stud, Kentucky
Fee in 2019: $110,000
Stallions by his sire include: Cairo Prince (Gr3), American Pharoah (2yo), Social Inclusion (yearlings), Classic Empire (foals), Empire Of D'Nile (foals), Midnight Storm (foals), River Dancer (foals), Shupanga (foals), Osiris Of The Nile (new)

AMERICAN PHAROAH (USA) – bay 2012

Pioneerof The Nile (USA)	Empire Maker (USA)	Unbridled (USA)
		Toussaud (USA)
	Star Of Goshen (USA)	Lord At War (ARG)
		Castle Eight (USA)
Littleprincessemma (USA)	Yankee Gentleman (USA)	Storm Cat (USA)
		Key Phrase (USA)
	Exclusive Rosette (USA)	Ecliptical (USA)
		Zetta Jet (USA)

SALES YEARLINGS OF 2018

Sold in Euros

Lashara (GB)

f - Marbre Rose (by Smart Strike) - Arqana - August - €850,000
f - Shawara (by Barathea) - Arqana - August - €750,000

Sold in US Dollars

c - Kindle (by Indian Charlie) - Keeneland - September - $2,200,000
c - Bsharpsonata (by Pulpit) - Keeneland - September - $1,400,000
f - Life At Ten (by Malibu Moon) - Fasig-Tipton Saratoga - August - $1,200,000
f - Pretty 'n Smart (by Beau Genius) - Keeneland - September - $1,200,000
c - Party Silks (by Touch Gold) - Fasig-Tipton Saratoga - August - $1,000,000

Feeling Funny (USA)   f - Funny Feeling (by Distorted Humor)
                          - Fasig-Tipton Saratoga - August -
                          $875,000

Good Fortune (USA)   c - Dancing Trieste (by Old Trieste) -
                          Keeneland - September - $800,000
                          c - Ragtime Hope (by Dixieland Band) -
                          Keeneland - September - $800,000
                          c - Up (by Galileo) - Keeneland -
                          September - $750,000
                          f - Mohini (by Galileo) - Keeneland -
                          September - $675,000
                          f - Beholden (by Cat Thief) - Fasig-
                          Tipton Saratoga - August - $625,000
                          c - Concinnous (by El Corredor) -
                          Keeneland - September - $600,000
                          f - Sweet N Discreet (by Discreet Cat) -
                          Keeneland - September - $600,000
                          c - Golden Sheba (by Coronado's
                          Quest) - Keeneland - September -
                          $550,000
                          c - Funfair (by More Than Ready) -
                          Fasig-Tipton Saratoga - August -
                          $525,000
                          c - Khancord Kid (by Lemon Drop
                          Kid) - Keeneland - September -
                          $500,000
                          c - True Feelings (by Latent Heat) -
                          Keeneland - September - $500,000
                          c - Meerkat Miss (by Giant's Causeway)
                          - Keeneland - September - $475,000
                          f - Burning Arch (by Arch) - Keeneland
                          - September - $450,000
                          f - Visions Of Annette (by Distorted
                          Humor) - Fasig-Tipton New York -
                          August - $450,000
                          c - Paradise Playgirl (by Speightstown) -
                          Keeneland - September - $435,000
                          f - Saint Bernadette (by Saint Ballado) -
                          Keeneland - September - $425,000

f - Maybellene (by Lookin At Lucky) -
Keeneland - September - $375,000
c - Wile Cat (by Storm Cat) - Keeneland
- September - $375,000
f - Baroness Amira (by Street Cry) -
Keeneland - September - $360,000
c - Harmony Lodge (by Hennessy) -
Keeneland - September - $350,000

Pharelli (USA)
c - Schiaparelli (by Ghoszapper) -
Keeneland - September - $340,000
f - Cat Moves (by Tale Of The Cat) -
Keeneland - September - $325,000
c - I O Ireland (by Giant's Causeway) -
Keeneland - September - $325,000
f - Ivanavinalot (by West Acre) -
Keeneland - September - $325,000
f - Margate Gardens (by Speightstown) -
Fasig-Tipton Saratoga - August -
$325,000
c - Gloat (by Mr Greeley) - Fasig-Tipton
Kentucky - October - $310,000
f - Intelyhente (by Smart Strike) -
Keeneland - September - $310,000
c - Danceinthesunlight (by A.P. Indy) -
Fasig-Tipton Kentucky - October -
$300,000
c - Global Finance (by End Sweep) -
Fasig-Tipton Saratoga - August -
$300,000
f - Mariel N Kathy (by Corinthian) -
Keeneland - September - $300,000
f - My Happy Face (by Tiz Wonderful) -
Keeneland - September - $300,000
f - Skyscape (by Marquetry) - Keeneland
- September - $300,000
f - Tap Of The Day (by Pulpit) -
Keeneland - September - $280,000
c - Tare Green (by Giant's Causeway) -
Keeneland - September - $275,000

Album (USA)

f - J Z Now (by Tiznow) - Fasig-Tipton
Saratoga - August - $260,000
c - Beautician (by Dehere) - Keeneland -
September - $250,000
c - Gilt (by Bernardini) - Keeneland -
September - $250,000
c - Jeweliana (by Smart Strike) - Fasig-
Tipton Saratoga - August - $235,000
f - Platinum (by Mineshaft) - Keeneland
- September - $220,000
c - Spice Island (by Tabasco Cat) -
Keeneland - September - $215,000
c - Retraceable (by Medaglia d'Oro) -
Keeneland - September - $210,000
c - Joyful Victory (by Tapit) - Keeneland
- September - $200,000
c - Our Love Tap (by Tapit) -
Keeneland - September - $200,000
f - She Be Classy (by Toccet) - Fasig-
Tipton Saratoga - August - $200,000
f - Yong Musician (by Yonaguska) -
Fasig-Tipton Kentucky - July - $200,000
c - Profess (by War Front) - Keeneland
- September - $160,000
f - Virginia Waters (by Kingmambo) -
Keeneland - September - $150,000
c - Placentia (by Bernardini) -
Keeneland - September - $135,000
f - Pulsating (by Pulpit) - Keeneland -
September - $135,000
f - Toast To Ashley (by First Defence) -
Ocala Breeders' Sales Company -
October - $130,000
c - Loudly (by War Front) - Keeneland -
September - $120,000
c - Parris Hill (by A.P. Indy) -
Keeneland - September - $115,000
c - Enhancing (by Forestry) - Fasig-
Tipton Kentucky - October - $100,000

I'm American Made (USA) f - More Hennessy (by Hennessy) - Keeneland - September - $100,000
c - Sea Queen (by Lemon Drop Kid) - Keeneland - September - $90,000
c - Ponche De Leona (by Ponche) - Keeneland - September - $80,000
c - P. S. U. Grad (by Harlan's Holiday) - Keeneland - September - $60,000
f - Iplaytricks (by Desert God) - Fasig-Tipton Kentucky - October - $30,000

Not Sold (inc. vendor buy-backs)

f - A. P. Dream (by A.P. Indy) - Fasig-Tipton Kentucky - October
f - Accusation (by Royal Academy) - Keeneland - September
f - Arch's Gal Edith (by Arch) - Keeneland - September
f - Bonnie Blue Flag (by Mineshaft) - Keeneland - September
f - Cherokee Queen (by Cherokee Run) - Keeneland - September

Envied (USA) f - Halljoy (by Halling) - Keeneland - September
c - Heart Of Paradise (by More Than Ready) - Keeneland - September
c - Hessonite (by Freud) - Fasig-Tipton Saratoga - August
c - J Z Warrior (by Harlan's Holiday) - Fasig-Tipton Saratoga - August
c - Kibosh (by Discreet Cat) - Keeneland - September
f - Light The City (by Street Sense) - Keeneland - September

Comeback (USA) c - Mighty Renee (by Maria's Mon) - Keeneland - September
c - Mo Chuisle (by Free House) - Keeneland - September
c - New Wave (by Tale Of The Cat) - Keeneland - September

14

AMERICAN PHAROAH (USA)

f - Seacrettina (by Sea Of Secrets) -
Keeneland - September
c - Star Sighting (by Malibu Moon) -
Keeneland - September
f - Stopshoppingdebbie (by Curlin) -
Keeneland - September
f - Theworldweknow (by Speightstown)
- Keeneland - September

15

ANJAAL (GB)

With so many stallions representing the Danehill, Green Desert, Galileo or other branches of the Northern Dancer (by Nearctic) male line, it is no surprise that a speedy colt from a different one should prove so popular when going to stud. Anjaal (by Bahamian Bounty) is a grandson of Cadeaux Genereux (by Young Generation), he has no Danzig blood in his pedigree, but he has Nureyev (by Northern Dancer) as his dam's grandsire. Nureyev was a three-parts brother to Sadler's Wells (by Northern Dancer), and so Anjaal is not an outcross for most horses from that line given that outcross – a term too often misused these days – means no duplicated ancestors within the first five generations of the pedigree.

He got off the mark at the second attempt as a juvenile, scoring by four lengths over five furlongs at Beverley in early June, and followed that with a narrow win in the Group 2 July Stakes at Newmarket. His only other outing that season resulted in a fourth-place finish behind War Command in the Group 1 Dewhurst Stakes. He ran five times as a three-year-old but was unplaced in four, and yet, with a three-quarter-length third to Es Que Love in the Group 2 Lennox Stakes the highlight of his campaign, he finished the year on a much higher Timeform rating than he'd achieved at two – 117 versus 107 – which suggests that many of his progeny may also be better as three-year-olds and older horses than the level they achieve at two.

The Rathasker Stud team member has a large first crop (145) to represent him and looks likely to get his best winners in the broad five-to-12-furlong range. The latter may surprise some, but this half-brother to a Czech National Hunt blacktype scorer is out of dual French middle-distance winner Ballymore Celebre (by Peintre Celebre) and from a family that has yielded blacktype horses over a wide range of distances. Her half-brother Nysaean (by Sadler's Wells) won the Group 3 Gallinule Stakes, two editions of the Group 3 Mooresbridge Stakes, and finished third in the Group 1 Tattersalls Gold Cup, whereas another sibling, Charme Slave (by Sicyos), won a listed sprint in France, and Celtic Cavalier (by Caerleon) was runner-up in the Group 1 National Stakes.

Their siblings also include Lili Cup (by Fabulous Dancer), and she is the dam of pattern-placed middle-distance stakes winner All The Aces (by Spartacus) and of Uruk (by Efisio), a sprint pattern winner whose descendants include Group 3 Prix Miesque heroine Dame Du Roi (by Dark Angel) and Group 2-placed French stayer Lucky Look (by Teofilo). Third dam Arme d'Or (by Armistice) was runner-up in both the Grand Prix de Deauville and Prix Maurice de Nieuil, the best of her offspring was Morold (by Sir Gaylord), a triple Grade 2 scorer from eight to 12 furlongs, and many of her most notable descendants also showed their best form in the 10-14 furlong range.

The dams of Anjaal's offspring may determine their prospects. His large initial crop size makes it likely he will have a lot of early-season two-year-old runners – some of whom may become winners – but if what he passes on is something of the distaff side of his pedigree rather than the five-to-eight-furlong potential of his sire, then those individuals will need a bit more time and distance, hence his potential to get capable performers over a wide range of trips.

SUMMARY DETAILS

Stood in 2016: Rathasker Stud, Ireland
Fee in 2016: €5,000
Career highlights: 2 wins inc July Stakes (Gr2), 3rd Lennox Stakes (Gr2)
Standing in 2019: Rathasker Stud, Ireland
Fee in 2019: €5,000
Stallions by his sire include: Pastoral Pursuits (Gr3), Goodricke (winners), Anjaal (2yo)

ANJAAL (GB) – chestnut 2011

	Cadeaux Genereux	Young Generation
Bahamian Bounty (GB)		Smarten Up
	Clarentia	Ballad Rock
		Laharden
	Peintre Celebre (USA)	Nureyev (USA)
Ballymore Celebre (IRE)		Peinture Bleue (USA)
	Irish Arms (FR)	Irish River (FR)
		Arme D'Or (FR)

ANJAAL (GB)

SALES YEARLINGS OF 2018

Sold in Euros

	chc - Lizzy's Township (by Delaware Township) - Goffs - October - €26,000
	chc - Nordkappe (by High Chaparral) - Tatts IRE - September - €22,000
Speriamo Bene (IRE)	chc - La Belle Maison (by Titus Livius) - Goffs - October - €21,000
	bc - Broken Applause (by Acclamation) - Arqana - October - €18,000
	chc - Fancy Vivid (by Galileo) - Tatts IRE - September - €18,000
	chc - Disprove (by Approve) - Tatts IRE - September - €17,000
	bc - Defensive Boast (by El Gran Senor) - Tatts IRE - September - €15,000 (p/s)
	chf - Dirtybirdie (by Diktat) - Tatts IRE - September - €15,000
	bf - Mia Madonna (by Motivator) - Tatts IRE - September - €15,000
	bc - Millport (by Zamindar) - Goffs - October - €15,000
	chc - Straight Sets (by Pivotal) - Tatts IRE - September - €13,500
	bc - Millport (by Zamindar) - Goffs - February - €12,500
	bc - She's Neat (by Frozen Power) - Tatts IRE - September - €12,000
	chf - Trading Places (by Dansili) - Goffs - November - €12,000
	chc - Disprove (by Approve) - Goffs - February - €11,000
	bc - Melatonia (by King Charlemagne) - Goffs - February - €11,000
	bc - Generous Gesture (by Fasliyev) - Tatts IRE - September - €10,000
	bc - Brazilian Breeze (by Invincible Spirit) - Goffs - November - €9,000

chc - Platinum Darling (by Iffraaj) -
Tatts IRE - September - €9,000
bf - Pescia (by Darshaan) - Goffs -
October - €8,000
chc - Petite Georgia (by Camacho) -
Tatts IRE - September - €8,000
bf - Twenty Questions (by Kyllachy) -
Tatts IRE - September - €8,000
bf - Belle Of The Blues (by Blues
Traveller) - Tatts IRE - September -
€7,000
bf - Wishyouwerehere (by
Footstepsinthesand) - Tatts IRE -
September - €6,500
bf - Tereed Elhawa (by Cadeaux
Genereux) - Tatts IRE - September -
€6,000
chc - Clytha (by Mark Of Esteem) -
Goffs - October - €5,500
bc - Tatamagouche (by Sadler's Wells) -
Tatts IRE - September - €5,500
bc - Magical Bupers (by Intikhab) -
Tatts IRE - September - €4,200
bc - Bank On Black (by Big Bad Bob) -
Tatts IRE - September - €4,000
bf - Life Rely (by Maria's Mon) - Goffs -
October - €4,000
bf - Russian Spirit (by Falbrav) - Goffs -
October - €4,000
chc - Coin From Heaven by Invincible
Spirit) - Goffs - October - €3,500
chf - Katayeb (by Machiavellian) - Goffs
- November - €3,500
bf - Comedic Art (by Dansili) - Goffs -
February - €3,000
chc - Piccelina (by Piccolo) - Tatts IRE -
September - €3,000
bc - Trebles (by Kenmare) - Goffs -
February - €3,000

20

chc - Turban Heights (by Golan) - Tatts
IRE - September - €3,000 (p/s)
chc - Dangerous Duo (by Intikhab) -
Goffs - November - €2,000
chf - Knowing Look (by Daylami) -
Goffs - November - €2,000
bf - Oratrix (by Oratorio) - Tatts IRE -
September - €2,000
chf - Kill With A Smile (by Tiger Hill) -
Goffs - November - €1,800
bc - Akariyda (by Salse) - Tatts IRE -
September - €1,500
bc - Apasiona (by Invincible Spirit) -
Tatts IRE - September - €1,500
bf - Wild Ocean (by Pivotal) - Goffs -
November - €1,200 (p/s)
chf - Allegrissimo (by Redback) - Tatts
IRE - September - €1,000
chf - Malory Towers (by Giant's
Causeway) - Goffs - November - €1,000

Sold in Guineas

chc - Just Devine (by Montjeu) -
Tattersalls - October - 100,000gns
chc - Vexatious (by Shamardal) -
Tattersalls - October - 78,000gns
chc - Malekat Jamal (by Dutch Art) -
Tattersalls - October - 45,000gns
Trumpets Call (IRE) chc - Yellow Trumpet (by Petong) -
Tattersalls - October - 40,000gns
Lady Latte (IRE) bf - Cappuccino (by Mujadil) -
Tattersalls - October - 38,000gns
Howtownstreet Harry (IRE) bc - Kathy Sun (by Intikhab) -
Tattersalls - October - 35,000gns
chc - Nijah (by Pivotal) - Tattersalls -
October - 28,000gns
On The Brightside (IRE) chc - Kardyls Hope (by Fath) -
Tattersalls - October - 25,000gns
Forgetful Agent (GB) chc - Bronze Star (by Mark Of Esteem)
- Tattersalls - October - 15,000gns

Castel Angelo (IRE)	chc - Solace (by Langfuhr) - Tattersalls - October - 8,000gns
	bc - La Chita Bonita (by Verglas) - Tattersalls - October - 7,000gns
	chf - Generous Heart (by Sakhee's Secret) - Tattersalls - October - 6,000gns
	bf - Glen Molly (by Danetime) - Tattersalls - October - 3,000gns

Sold in Pounds

Emily's Delight (IRE)	bc - Pearly Brooks (by Efisio) - Goffs UK - August - £30,000
	chf - Masela (by Medicean) - Goffs UK - August - £26,000
Elpheba (IRE)	bf - Broadway Musical (by Exceed And Excel) - Goffs UK - August - £25,000
	chc - Clann Force (by Kyllachy) - Goffs UK - August - £25,000
Midnight Mimosa (IRE)	chf - Miss Prim (by Case Law) - Goffs UK - August - £20,000
	chc - Emma Dora (by Medaglia d'Oro) - Tatts IRE Ascot - September - £15,000
	chc - Kitty Softpaws (by Royal Applause) - Goffs UK - August - £15,000
	bc - Princess Banu (by Oasis Dream) - Tatts IRE Ascot - September - £15,000
	bf - Miss Inferno (by Tagula) - Goffs UK - August - £10,500
	bc - Ho Hey (by Paco Boy) - Goffs UK - August - £7,000
	chc - Vaughn Got Style (by Champs Elysees) - Goffs UK - August - £7,000
	bc - Effige (by Oratorio) - Goffs UK - August - £6,000
	bc - Danza Nera (by Dansili) - Goffs UK - August - £5,000

ANJAAL (GB)

	bc - Mistress Of Rome (by Holy Roman Emperor) - Goffs UK - August - £5,000 (p/s)
Bettys Hope (GB)	bf - Miss Poppy (by Averti) - Tatts IRE Ascot - September - £3,000

Not Sold (inc. vendor buy-backs)

chc - Abbotsfield (by Sakhee's Secret) - Tattersalls - October

bc - Akariyda (by Salse) - Goffs - February

chc - Bells Of Ireland (by Machiavellian) - Goffs - November

chc - Bulgaden Cross (by Dutch Art) - Goffs - November

bf - Bush Maiden (by Among Men) - Goffs - November

bf - Candlelight (by Zebedee) - Goffs - November

chf - Chinese Democracy (by Proud Citizen) - Goffs - November

bf - Comedic Art (by Dansili) - Goffs UK - October

chc - Dance Bid (by Authorized) - Goffs UK - August

chc - Dancing Lauren (by Oratorio) - Goffs - February

chc - Dancing Lauren (by Oratorio) - Tatts IRE - September

chc - Elayoon (by Danzig) - Tattersalls - October

bf - Gabriellina Klon (by Ashkalani) - Tatts IRE - November

bf - Gin And Slim (by Dark Angel) - Goffs - February

bc - Gregorys Girl (by Oratorio) - Tatts IRE - September

chc - Hazardous (by Night Shift) - Goffs - October

23

Captain Corcoran (IRE) bc - Hms Pinafore (by Singspiel) - Goffs UK - August
bf - Holamo (by Montjeu) - Goffs - February
bf - Holamo (by Montjeu) - Goffs - November
bc - Houlgate (by Mount Nelson) - Tatts IRE - September
bf - Jallaissine (by College Chapel) - Goffs - October
bc - Kano's Ghirl (by Kodiac) - Goffs - November
bc - Ladytown (by Bertolini) - Tatts IRE - September
brc - Little Italy (by Proud Citizen) - Tatts IRE - September
bc - Melatonia (by King Charlemagne) - Goffs UK - August
bc - Mirandasister (by Titus Livius) - Tatts IRE - September
chf - Mymoonlightdancer (by Danehill Dancer) - Goffs - November
chf - Porcelana (by Highest Honor) Tatts IRE Ascot - November
bc - Prisca (by Holy Roman Emperor) - Goffs - February
bc - Prisca (by Holy Roman Emperor) - Tatts IRE Ascot - September
bf - Queen Althea (by Bach) - Goffs - November
bc - Rapparee (by Red Ransom) - Goffs - November
chf - Regresa A Mi (by Spartacus) - Goffs UK - October
chf - Riviera Romance (by Zamindar) - Goffs - November
bc - Safiya Song (by Intikhab) - Goffs - November
bf - Sampers (by Exceed And Excel) - Goffs - November

ANJAAL (GB)

chf - Sea Regatta (by Hurricane Run) -
Tatts IRE Ascot - November
bf - Shahmina (by Danehill) - Goffs -
November
bf - She Runs (by Sheyrann) - Goffs -
November
bf - So Dandy (by Oratorio) - Goffs -
November
chf - Sororal (by Dream Ahead) - Goffs
- November
bc - Standinthesunlight (by Paco Boy) -
Goffs - November
chf - Suedehead (by Cape Cross) -
Tattersalls - October
bc - Takaliya (by Darshaan) - Tatts IRE
- September
chf - Tiger Royale (by Tiger Hill) -
Goffs - November
bc - Trebles (by Kenmare) - Baden-
Baden - May
bf - Vivacious Way (by Holy Roman
Emperor) - Goffs - November
bf - Without Doubt (by Clodovil) -
Goffs - November
bc - Zahenda (by Exceed And Excel) -
Goffs - February
bc - Zahenda (by Exceed And Excel) -
Tatts IRE - September
bc - Zalanga (by Azamour) - Goffs -
October

FRESHMAN SIRES OF 2019

BRAZEN BEAU (AUS)

The mighty Danzig (by Northern Dancer) sire yielded two powerful branches, namely those forged by the classic-placed Group 1 sprint stars Danehill and Green Desert. (War Front may forge a third one.) Now we are seeing early signs that Green Desert's lineage is producing three branches of its own – those headed by Oasis Dream, Cape Cross, and Invincible Spirit. The latter's early stallion sons feature the Group 1 sires Lawman and I Am Invincible, and it is the second one of those who has given us international sprint ace and young Dalham Hall Stud reverse-shuttle stallion Brazen Beau.

A six-furlong Group 2 scorer in a juvenile season that culminated in a head second in a mile Group 1 contest, he went on to take the Group 1 Coolmore Stud Stakes over the former trip, chased home Lankan Rupee in the Group 1 Lightning Stakes, easily beat Chautauqua in the Group 1 Newmarket Handicap, and then chased home Undrafted in the Group 1 Diamond Jubilee Stakes.

This Timeform 126-rated sprinter is the best of a handful of stakes winners in the first four generations of his pedigree, but his fifth dam is the classic-placed Canadian star Windy Answer (by Windfields), the mare who gave us Ciboulette (by Chop Chop). In addition to being the dam of leading sire Night Shift (by Northern Dancer), the stakes-winning Ciboulette was responsible for Barachois (by Northern Dancer), Somfas (by What A Pleasure) and champion Fanfreluche (by Northern Dancer).

So, although they are remotely connected to him, Brazen Beau comes from a branch of the family of notable sires L'Enjoleur (by Buckpasser), Flying Spur (by Danehill), Encosta De Lago (by Fairy King), and Holy Roman Emperor (by Danehill), as well as many others who have sired blacktype scorers. Interestingly, the latter include Group 2 Temple Stakes winner Snaadee (by Danzig), the broodmare sire of Brazen Beau, which makes the young stallion inbred 5x5 to the aforementioned Windy Answer. He is also inbred 4x3 to Danzig, 4x3 to Bletchingly, and 5x4 to Nearctic.

Brazen Beau should be capable of getting some smart two-year-olds in Europe, in addition to some high-class sprinters and milers aged three and upwards, and it will be interesting to see how the northern hemisphere side of his career turns out. The southern hemisphere part of his career is already underway and, at the time of writing, he has been represented by listed scorer Accession (dam by More Than Ready), Group 2-placed Tassort (dam by Exceed And Excel), and listed-placed First Dawn (dam by Danehill) among his first Australian two-year-olds. His second crop 'down under' includes yearlings that made up to A$800,000 at the recent Inglis Premier Sale.

SUMMARY DETAILS

Stood in 2016: Dalham Hall Stud, England
Fee in 2016: £10,000
Career highlights: 5 wins inc Newmarket Handicap (Gr1), Coolmore Stud Stakes (Gr1), Bollinger Champagne Classic (Gr2), Roman Consul Stakes (Gr2), 2nd Diamond Jubilee Stakes (Gr1), Black Caviar Lightning Stakes (Gr1), J J Atkins Stakes (Gr1), Sires' Produce Stakes (Gr2)
Standing in 2019: Dalham Hall Stud, England
Fee in 2019: £7,000
Stallions by his sire include: Brazen Beau (2yo), Super One (2yo), Hellbent (foals), Kobayashi (foals), Overshare (foals)

BRAZEN BEAU (AUS) – brown 2011

I Am Invincible (AUS)	Invincible Spirit (IRE)	Green Desert (USA)
		Rafha
	Cannarelle (AUS)	Canny Lad (AUS)
		Countess Pedrille (AUS)
Sansadee (AUS)	Snaadee (USA)	Danzig (USA)
		Somfas (USA)
	Sansapa (AUS)	Bletchingly (AUS)
		Nearctic Answer (CAN)

SALES YEARLINGS OF 2018
Sold in Euros

bc - Tara's Force (by Acclamation) - Arqana - August - €130,000
b/brf - Cloudspin (by Storm Cat) - Goffs - October - €40,000
bc - Veiled Beauty (by Royal Academy) - Goffs - February - €40,000

Our Lad (GB) brc - Our Gal (by Kyllachy) - Tatts IRE
- September - €36,000
bc - Secret Liaison (by Dandy Man) -
Tatts IRE - September - €33,000
bc - Sugar Blossom (by Marju) - Tatts
IRE - September - €15,000 (p/s)
bc - Out Of Thanks (by Sadler's Wells) -
Arqana - August - €12,000
bc - Malpas Missile (by Elusive City) -
Baden-Baden - August - €8,000
bc - Snakestone (by Sakhee) - Goffs -
November - €8,000
bc - She's A Pistol (by Danehill Dancer)
- Tatts IRE - September - €5,000

Sold in Guineas

bc - Rose Kazan (by Teofilo) -
Tattersalls - October - 100,000gns
Bold Suitor (GB) bc - Samasana (by Redback) - Tattersalls
- October - 78,000gns
He's A Keeper (IRE) b/grc- Silver Grey (by Chineur) -
Tattersalls - October - 67,000gns
Silver Machine (GB) grf - Blue Crest (by Verglas) - Tattersalls
- October - 55,000gns
bc - Celestial Empire (by Empire
Maker) - Tattersalls - October -
55,000gns
Brash (GB) bc - Jaiyana (by Dansili) - Tattersalls -
October - 50,000gns
bc - Point Of Control (by Pivotal) -
Tattersalls - October - 50,000gns
bc - Netta (by Barathea) - Tattersalls -
October - 47,000gns
bc - Wigan Lane (by Kheleyf) -
Tattersalls - October - 45,000gns
Proper Beau (GB) bc - Olivia Grace (by Pivotal) -
Tattersalls - October - 34,000gns
Dubai Station (GB) bc - Princess Guest (by Iffraaj) -
Tattersalls - October - 30,000gns

	bf - Sharp Terms (by Kris) - Tattersalls - October - 20,000gns
Qaf (GB)	bc - Camelopardalis (by Tobougg) - Tattersalls - October - 19,000gns
	bc - Albany Rose (by Noverre) - Tattersalls - October - 18,000gns
Alsukar (GB)	bf - Three Sugars (by Starcraft) - Tattersalls - October - 16,000gns
Huraa (GB)	bf - Hakuraa (by Elnadim) - Tattersalls - October - 12,000gns
	bc - Shy Appeal (by Barathea) - Tattersalls - October - 11,000gns
Criseyde (GB)	bf - Flemish School (by Dutch Art) - Tattersalls - October - 9,000gns
	brf - Powerfulstorm (by Bertolini) - Tattersalls - November - 6,500gns
	bc - Nouveau Foret (by Myboycharlie) - Tattersalls - October - 5,500gns
	bc - Vespasia (by Medicean) - Tattersalls - October - 5,000gns (p/s)

Sold in Pounds

Spurofthemoment (IRE)	bf - Royal Blush (by Royal Applause) - Goffs UK - August - £100,000
Asdaf (IRE)	bc - Eclaircie (by Thunder Gulch) - Goffs UK - August - £90,000
Mr Beau Blue (GB)	brc - Precious Secret (by Fusaichi Pegasus) - Goffs UK - August - £80,000
One Colour (IRE)	bc - My Lucky Liz (by Exceed And Excel) - Goffs UK - August - £70,000
	bc - Moonlight Mystery (by Pivotal) - Goffs UK - August - £50,000
Cupid's Beau (GB)	bc - Oilinda (by Nayef) - Goffs UK - August - £40,000
	bc - Posy Fossil (by Malibu Moon) - Goffs UK - August - £35,000
	bc - Maziona (by Dansili) - Tatts IRE Ascot - September - £32,000
Coast Ofalfujairah (IRE)	bc - Khameela (by Equiano) - Goffs UK - August - £26,000

	brc - Break Time (by Dansili) - Goffs UK - August - £20,000
Brazen Safa (GB)	bf - Insaaf (by Averti) - Goffs UK - August - £20,000
Puffthemagicdragon (GB)	bc - Marmot Bay (by Kodiac) - Goffs UK - August - £19,000
	brf - Miramont (by Iffraaj) - Goffs UK - August - £10,000
	bf - Sweet Wind Music (by Zamindar) - Tatts IRE Ascot - September - £10,000
	bf - Showstoppa (by Showcasing) - Goffs UK - August - £8,000

Not Sold (inc. vendor buy-backs)

	bf - Coz I Do (by Pivotal) - Tattersalls - February
	blf - Dreamily (by New Approach) - Tatts IRE Ascot - September
	brf - Lovellian (by Machiavellian) - Goffs UK - August
Brazen Sheila (GB)	bf - Sail Home (by Mizzen Mast) - Tattersalls - October
	bc - Tanda Tula (by Alhaarth) - Goffs UK - August
	bc - Virginia Hall (by Medicean) - Goffs UK - August
	bc - Wigan Lane (by Kheleyf) - Goffs - February
	bf - Zeyada (by Marju) - Tattersalls - February
	bf - Zeyada (by Marju) - Goffs UK - October
	bf - Zeyran (by Galileo) - Goffs UK - August
	brf - Ziraun (by Cadeaux Genereux) - Tattersalls - October

FRESHMAN SIRES OF 2019

CABLE BAY (IRE)

Two of the factors that we consider when examining the future potential of any stallion are his male line and the presence or absence of successful sires within the distaff side of his family. In the case of Highclere Stud's talented six-to-eight-furlong performer Cable Bay, we have a horse who passes both of those tests with flying colours.

He is a son of Group 1 winning sprinter and leading international sire Invincible Spirit (by Green Desert), and so is by the horse who gave us Group 1 sires Lawman and I Am Invincible, among others who have come up with stakes and pattern winners. His dam, Rose De France (by Diktat), is a half-sister to the notable broodmare Moyesii (by Diesis) – the dam of Group 1 scorers Kirklees (by Jade Robbery) and Mastery (by Sulamani) – and although it remains to be seen how that mare's Group 1-winning grandson Mukhadram (by Shamardal) will be viewed in the coming years, members of the first crop by that young Nunnery Stud stallion have caught the eye. They are now three-year-olds, they include last year's listed-placed winner Gloves Lynch and also A Bit Special, a US-based filly who has won four of her first five starts including a mile Grade 3 contest at Gulfstream Park. The William Haggas-trained and Derby-entered colt Jahbath has also won four from five at the time of writing, those Polytrack and Fibresand wins coming by an aggregate margin of almost 15 lengths.

What stands out, however, concerning the stallion potential of both that horse and Cable Bay is that Rose De France and Moyesii are daughters of star sprinter Cherokee Rose (by Dancing Brave). The fastest representative of her Timeform 140-rated sire, she won the Group 1 Sprint Cup and Group 1 Prix Maurice de Gheest, she was runner-up in the Group 1 Prix de l'Abbaye de Longchamp, and she is a half-sister to Volksraad (by Green Desert). He was lightly raced and earned his blacktype when third in the Group 2 Challenge Stakes over seven furlongs, but he went on to become a prolific champion sire in New Zealand. He and Cable Bay are somewhat closely related.

There are plenty of other talented horses under the various branches of just these first three generations of the pedigree, but they do not tell us anything more about this young stallion's potential.

Cable Bay got 109 foals in his first crop – so he won't be short of representation – and it seems likely that some of his offspring could do well as juveniles, mostly in the second half of the season. He was runner-up in each of the Group 1 Dewhurst Stakes, Group 2 Richmond Stakes and Group 3 Somerville Tattersall Stakes at that age. His top wins came in the Group 2 Challenge Stakes and Group 3 John of Gaunt Stakes – over seven furlongs – as a four-year-old, and so his best results are likely to come with his three-year-olds and older horses, in the six-to-10-furlong range. There is every reason to hope that his top offspring will surpass his Timeform rating of 119.

SUMMARY DETAILS

Stood in 2016: Highclere Stud, England
Fee in 2016: £6,500
Career highlights: 3 wins inc Challenge Stakes (Gr2), John of Gaunt Stakes (Gr3), 2nd Dewhurst Stakes (Gr1), Challenge Stakes (Gr2), Richmond Stakes (Gr2), Somerville Tattersall Stakes (Gr3), 3rd Summer Mile Stakes (Gr2), Champagne Stakes (Gr2), Gladness Stakes (Gr3)
Standing in 2019: Highclere Stud, England
Fee in 2019: £6,500
Stallions by his sire include: I Am Invincible (Gr1), Lawman (Gr1), Kingman (Gr2), Zebedee (Gr2), Born To Sea (Gr3), Charm Spirit (Gr3), Vale Of York (Gr3), Captain Marvelous (L), Mayson (L), Swiss Spirit (winners), Cable Bay (2yo), Ajaya (yearlings), Life Force (yearlings), Shalaa (yearlings), Territories (yearlings), National Defense (foals), Profitable (foals), Shaiban (foals), Mr Owen (new)

CABLE BAY (IRE) – bay 2011

Invincible Spirit (IRE)	Green Desert (USA)	Danzig (USA)
		Foreign Courier (USA)
	Rafha	Kris
		Eljazzi
Rose De France (IRE)	Diktat (GB)	Warning
		Arvola (GB)
	Cherokee Rose (IRE)	Dancing Brave (USA)
		Celtic Assembly (USA)

SALES YEARLINGS OF 2018

Sold in Euros

Electric Ladyland (IRE)	bf - Conversational (by Thousand Words) - Goffs - October - €35,000
Isabeau (IRE)	bf - Semblance (by Pivotal) - Goffs - October - €30,000
	bc - Euroceleb (by Peintre Celebre) - Goffs - October - €26,000
	bf - Spectacular Show (by Spectrum) - Goffs - October - €25,000
	bc - High Tan (by High Chaparral) - Tatts IRE - September - €22,000
	brf - Ebony Street (by Street Cry) - Goffs - October - €18,000
	bc - Phoenix Clubs (by Red Clubs) - Tatts IRE - September - €9,000
	bc - On Wings Of Love (by Hawk Wing) - Tatts IRE - September - €7,500
	bf - Puff Pastry (by Pivotal) - Goffs - February - €5,500
	bc - Dona Sola (by Iffraaj) - Tatts IRE - September - €5,000
	bf - Ballet Move (by Oasis Dream) - Goffs - October - €3,000

Sold in Guineas

	bf - Triton Dance (by Hector Protector) - Tattersalls - October - 55,000gns
Cable Speed (IRE)	bc - Hear My Cry (by Giant's Causeway) - Tattersalls - October - 30,000gns
	bf - Jacaranda Ridge (by Indian Ridge) - Tattersalls - October - 28,000gns
	brc - Hewayaat (by Cape Cross) - Tattersalls - October - 25,000gns
	bc - Angels Wings (by Dark Angel) - Tattersalls - October - 21,000gns
	bc - Demisemiquaver (by Singspiel) - Tattersalls - October - 21,000gns
	bc - Fisadara (by Nayef) - Tattersalls - October - 17,000gns

Front Of Line (GB)

bf - Grand Depart (by Royal Applause) - Tattersalls - October - 17,000gns
bc - Broughtons Flight (by Hawk Wing) - Tattersalls - October - 16,000gns
bf - Mutheera (by Oasis Dream) - Tattersalls - October - 10,000gns
bf - Carved Emerald (by Pivotal) - Tattersalls - October - 9,000gns
bc - Lyric Art (by Red Ransom) - Tattersalls - October - 9,000gns
bf - First Approval (by Royal Applause) - Tattersalls - October - 8,500gns
bf - Pivotal Drive (by Pivotal) - Tattersalls - October - 8,000gns
bf - Lady Macduff (by Iffraaj) - Tattersalls - October - 6,500gns
bc - Blissamore (by Kyllachy) - Tattersalls - October - 6,000gns
bf - Read Federica (by Fusaichi Pegasus) - Tattersalls - October - 5,500gns
bf - Guiletta (by Dalakhani) - Tattersalls - October - 4,500gns
bc - Palais Polaire (by Polar Falcon) - Tattersalls - October - 4,500gns
bf - Across The Galaxy (by Cape Cross) - Tattersalls - February - 4,000gns
bc - Brigantian (by Makfi) - Tattersalls - November - 3,000gns
bc - Clinet (by Docksider) - Tattersalls - February - 2,000gns
bc - Touching (by Kheleyf) - Tattersalls - October - 2,000gns
bf - Marigay's Magic (by Rock Of Gibraltar) - Tattersalls - October - 1,800gns
bf - Decorative (by Danehill Dancer) - Tattersalls - February - 800gns

36

Sold in Pounds

Al Sakeet (GB)
bc - Coin A Phrase (by Dubawi) - Goffs UK - August - £150,000
bc - Hadeeya (by Oratorio) - Goffs UK - August - £110,000

St Ives (GB)
bc - Galaktea (by Statue Of Liberty) - Goffs UK - August - £90,000

Triple Glory (GB)
bf - Triple Star (by Royal Applause) - Goffs UK - August - £62,000

Southern Dancer (GB)
bc - Mambo Halo (by Southern Halo) - Goffs UK - August - £60,000
bc - Alzahra (by Exceed And Excel) - Goffs UK - August - £38,000

Separate (GB)
bf - Miss Moses (by Gulch) - Goffs UK - August - £30,000
bc - Mill Point (by Champs Elysees) - Goffs UK - August - £22,000
bf - Breath Of Dawn (by Dubawi) - Goffs UK - October - £15,000
bc - Kibara (by Sadler's Wells) - Goffs UK - August - £15,000
bc - Warden Rose (by Compton Place) - Goffs UK - August - £13,000
bc - Local Fancy (by Bahamian Bounty) - Goffs UK - August - £12,000
bc - Tarando (by Equiano) - Goffs UK - August - £11,000 (p/s)

Rushcutters Bay (GB)
bc - Kicker Rock (by Fastnet Rock) - Goffs UK - August - £10,000 (p/s)
bc - Ribbon Royale (by Royal Applause) - Tatts IRE Ascot - September - £9,500
bf - Excel Yourself (by Exceed And Excel) - Goffs UK - August - £8,000 (p/s)
bf - Musicora (by Acclamation) - Goffs UK - October - £6,000
bf - Tamara Moon (by Acclamation) - Goffs UK - August - £6,000

Light Bay (GB)
bf - Key Light (by Acclamation) - Tatts IRE Ascot - September - £5,000

bf - Siena Gold (by Key Of Luck) - Goffs UK - August - £5,000
grf - Ghedi (by Aussie Rules) - Goffs UK - October - £3,500
grf - Silver Rainbow (by Starspangledbanner) - Tatts IRE Ascot - September - £3,000
bf - Bubbly Ballerina (by Footstepsinthesand) - Tatts IRE Ascot - September - £2,500
bf - Puff Pastry (by Pivotal) - Goffs UK - August - £2,000
bc - Atalis (by Holy Roman Emperor) - Tatts IRE Ascot - September - £800

Not Sold (inc. vendor buy-backs)

brc - Ashwell Rose (by Anabaa) - Tatts IRE - September
bc - Basque Beauty (by Nayef) - Tattersalls - October
bf - Breath Of Dawn (by Dubawi) - Tatts IRE Ascot - March
bf - Divine Power (by Kyllachy) - Tatts IRE Ascot - September
brf - Dos Lunas (by Galileo) - Goffs UK - August
bf - Flirtinaskirt (by Avonbridge) - Tatts IRE Ascot - September
grf - Ghedi (by Aussie Rules) - Tatts IRE Ascot - September
bc - Jessie's Spirit (by Clodovil) - Tattersalls - October
c - Kitba (by New Approach) - Goffs - February
bf - Leap Of Joy (by Canford Cliffs) - Goffs - October

Tomfre (GB) bc - Kurtanella (by Pastoral Pursuits) - Tatts IRE Ascot - December
bf - La Noe (by Nayef) - Goffs - October

CABLE BAY (IRE)

bc - Mahatta (by Halling) - Tatts IRE
Ascot - September
bc - Mimiteh (by Maria's Mon) - Goffs
UK - August
bf - Musicora (by Acclamation) - Tatts
IRE Ascot - March
bf - Royal Confidence (by Royal
Applause) - Tatts IRE Ascot -
December
bc - Zambujeiro (by Dutch Art) - Tatts
IRE - September
bc - Zambujeiro (by Dutch Art) -
Tattersalls - November

CAPPELLA SANSEVERO (GB)

Bridge House Stud stallion Cappella Sansevero (by Showcasing) was among the best early-season juveniles of his year, winning the Listed Marble Hill Stakes and chasing home The Wow Signal in the Group 2 Coventry Stakes, but he also held his form through to the end of the year. He was only by beaten by half a length and a short-head when third to Dick Whittington and Kool Company in the Group 1 Phoenix Stakes on soft ground at the Curragh, three weeks before taking the Group 3 Round Tower Stakes on good-to-yielding at the same course and distance. Then, in mid-October, he was a one-and-three-quarter-length fourth to Charming Thought in the Group 1 Middle Park Stakes at Newmarket.

Timeform rated him 109 at two and 104 at three, the latter representing his close sixth-place finish in the seven-furlong Ballycorus Stakes at Leopardstown. That proved to be his final start and came just weeks after two unplaced classic attempts at a mile.

He is by the sire of six-furlong Group 1 stars Quiet Reflection and Advertise, he got 56 foals in his first crop and is the first offspring of the winning Madam President (by Royal Applause). She is a half-sister to Group 2 Ribblesdale Stakes runner-up Eldalil (by Singspiel), her dam is one-time scorer White House (by Pursuit Of Love), and the next dam is the dual two-year-old winner Much Too Risky (by Bustino). That mare is the dam of the Group 1-placed middle-distance Group 2 winners Little Rock (by Warning) and Whitewater Affair (by Machiavellian), classic-placed dual middle-distance Group 3 scorer Short Skirt (by Diktat) and three other blacktype horses.

Whitewater Affair has been an outstanding broodmare in Japan where she has been represented by Group 1 Yasuda Kinen scorer Asakusa Den'en (by Singspiel) and the even more talented Victoire Pisa (by Neo Universe). A champion at three and four years of age, he won the Group 1 Satsuki Sho (Japanese 2000 Guineas), Group 1 Arima Kinen, and Group 1 Dubai World Cup, he was placed in the Group 1 Tokyo Yushun (Japanese Derby) and Group 1 Japan Cup, and the early runners by the Shadai Stallion Station resident feature classic heroine Jeweler.

If you go back another generation, then you will find that Much Too Risky's siblings include Group 1 Irish St Leger winner Arctic Owl (by Most Welcome) and Group 1 Sydney Cup scorer Marooned (by Mill Reef), further evidence of the strong stamina influence that this family had for so long.

However, Cappella Sansevero represents an emerging speed branch of the line, both as a grandson of sprint champion and classic sire Oasis Dream (by Green Desert) and out of a mare who represents a Royal Applause (by Waajib) – Pursuit Of Love (by Groom Dancer) cross. His speed, his precocity, and the more immediate elements of his pedigree combine to paint a picture of a young stallion who is like to do well with all age groups, getting his best runners in the five-to-eight-furlong range. The presence of a successful stallion in the distaff side of his family is also encouraging, even if that horse's talents are notably different and his actual relationship remote.

SUMMARY DETAILS

Stood in 2016: Bridge House Stud, Ireland
Fee in 2016: €4,500
Career highlights: 4 wins inc Round Tower Stakes (Gr3),
Marble Hill Stakes (L), 2nd Coventry Stakes (Gr2), 3rd Phoenix
Stakes (Gr1)
Standing in 2019: Bridge House Stud, Ireland
Fee in 2019: €4,000
Stallions by his sire include: Cappella Sansevero (2yo), Tasleet
(new)

CAPPELLA SANSEVERO (GB) – bay 2012

Showcasing (GB)	Oasis Dream (GB)	Green Desert (USA)
		Hope (IRE)
	Arabesque (GB)	Zafonic (USA)
		Prophecy (IRE)
Madam President (GB)	Royal Applause (GB)	Waajib
		Flying Melody
	White House (GB)	Pursuit Of Love (GB)
		Much Too Risky

SALES YEARLINGS OF 2018

Sold in Euros

	bc - Mean Lae (by Johannesburg) - Goffs - February - €45,000
	bc - Seraphina (by Pips Pride) - Goffs - October - €40,000
Salkeev (IRE)	bf - Hadya (by Teofilo) - Tatts IRE - September - €30,000
	bc - Just Like Ivy (by Street Cry) - Goffs - February - €13,500
	bf - Dissonance (by Rossini) - Tatts IRE - September - €6,500
	chc - Artistic Dancer (by Dutch Art) - Goffs - November - €5,500
	chc - Batuta (by New Approach) - Tatts IRE - September - €4,200
	chc - Burn The Bond (by Monsieur Bond) - Goffs - November - €4,000
	bc - Maya de La Luz (by Selkirk) - Goffs - November - €4,000
	bf - Labba (by Tiger Hill) - Goffs - November - €2,000
	bf - Chrissycross (by Cape Cross) - Goresbridge - October - €1,000
	bf - Ja One (by Acclamation) - Goffs - November - €1,000
	chf - Lady Magdalena (by Invincible Spirit) - Goffs - November - €1,000
	bc - Mississipi Delta (by Cape Cross) - Goffs - November - €1,000

Sold in Guineas

Pierre Lapin (IRE)   bc - Beatrix Potter (by Cadeaux Genereux) - Tattersalls - October - 140,000gns

Sold in Pounds

Panic Room (IRE)   brc - Varnay (by Machiavellian) - Goffs UK - August - £60,000

bc - Almatlaie (by Elusive Quality) -
Goffs UK - August - £25,000
chf - City Vaults Girl (by Oratorio) -
Tatts IRE Ascot - September - £10,000

Not Sold (inc. vendor buy-backs)

bf - Annellis (by Diesis) - Goffs -
November
chc - Australia Fair (by Pivotal) - Goffs
- November
bf - Babycakes (by Marju) - Arqana -
August
bc - Candycakes (by Cape Cross) - Tatts
IRE - September
bf - Chennai (by Mozart) - Goffs -
November
bf - Common Cause (by Polish Patriot)
- Goffs - October
bf - Confirm (by In The Wings) - Goffs
- November
chc - Dane Blue (by Danehill Dancer) -
Goffs - November
bc - Fascination Street (by Mujadil) -
Goffs - November
bc - Gift Of Fantasy (by Authorized) -
Tatts IRE - September
chf - Heloisa (by Bachelor Duke) -
Goffs - November
bf - Kyrielle (by Medicean) - Goffs -
November
bc - Madame Nobel (by Alfred Nobel) -
Goffs - November
bf - Midnight Muscida (by Kodiac) -
Goffs - November
bf - Pink Plum (by Mastercraftsman) -
Goffs - November
bc - Stroll On (by Exceed And Excel) -
Goffs - November

CAPPELLA SANSEVERO (GB)

DUE DILIGENCE (USA)

We have, for a long time now, been able to talk about there being two major branches of the mighty Danzig (by Northern Dancer) sire line, and there are no signs yet that those Danehill and Green Desert lines may be dimming. There was, however, always the possibility that one of his late sons might step forward to join that pair, and both Hard Spun and War Front emerged as the contenders. It is still too early to claim either is the progenitor of a line, but with Group/Grade 1-siring stallions The Factor and Declaration Of War among his initial sire sons and his 2018 freshmen including blacktype sire War Command, the signs are positive that Claiborne Farm's Grade 2-winning sprinter War Front may indeed achieve the feat.

Due Diligence is another of his talented sons, achieving a 120 rating from Timeform as a three-year-old despite never winning in pattern company, and the Whitsbury Manor Stud resident has been a popular choice with breeders. There are 79 in his first crop.

He began his career in the USA and was an eight-length debut winner over five and a half furlongs on turf at Saratoga in mid-August of his juvenile season. He was beaten by that same margin when fourth to subsequent Grade 1 star Bobby's Kitten in an eight-and-a-half-furlong Grade 3 at Belmont Park on his only other outing for the Todd Pletcher stable, and a few months later he crossed the Atlantic to join the team at Ballydoyle. He was third in a seven-furlong listed contest at Dundalk first time out, followed a six-furlong Naas handicap score with an easy listed success over that course and distance almost three weeks later, and then chased home Slade Power in the Group 1 Diamond Jubilee Stakes at Royal Ascot. That was to prove a career highlight as he finished unplaced in four runs at four, on his return from a lengthy absence.

A $190,000 Keeneland September Yearling Sale graduate whose dam, Bema (by Pulpit), won an eight-and-a-half-furlong listed contest at Aqueduct, Due Diligence is out of a half-sister to the dam of mile Grade 2 scorer Dancinginherdreams (by Tapit) and to the grandam of last year's Group 1 2000 Guineas runner-up Tip Two Win (by Dark Angel). His grandam, Dhaka (by

Icecapade), is one of three stakes winners out of Cloudy Day Sunny (by Buckaroo), who is a winning half-sister to Grade 1 Oak Tree Invitational Handicap and Grade 1 Hollywood Invitational Handicap scorer Both Ends Burning (by Nalees Man). This is a branch of the family of New Zealand champion Sangster (by Savabeel) whose Group 1 wins include the Victoria Derby. If you go back another generation, then you will find that Star Game (by Pia Star) – the fourth dam of Due Diligence – was a half-sister to Grade 1 Swaps Stakes winner Hyperborean (by Icecapade), who was somewhat closely related to Dhaka.

Due Diligence looks a likely candidate to get most of his juvenile winners in the second half of the season and to become a source of horses who prove best in the broad five-to-10-furlong range as three-year-olds and older horses.

SUMMARY DETAILS
Stood in 2016: Whitsbury Manor Stud, England
Fee in 2016: £6,500
Career highlights: 3 wins inc Lackan Stakes (L), 2nd Diamond Jubilee Stakes (Gr1), 3rd Patton Stakes (L)
Standing in 2019: Whitsbury Manor Stud, England
Fee in 2019: £4,000
Stallions by his sire include: Declaration Of War (Gr1), The Factor (Gr1), State Of Play (Gr2), Data Link (L), Soldat (L), War Command (L), Due Diligence (2yo), Jack Milton (2yo), Summer Front (2yo), Air Force Blue (yearlings), Hit A Bomb (yearlings), War Correspondent (yearlings), War Dancer (yearlings), American Patriot (foals), Lancaster Bomber (new), U S Navy Flag (new)

DUE DILIGENCE (USA) – bay 2011

War Front (USA)	Danzig (USA)	Northern Dancer (CAN)
		Pas De Nom (USA)
	Starry Dreamer (USA)	Rubiano (USA)
		Lara's Star (USA)
Bema (USA)	Pulpit (USA)	A.P. Indy (USA)
		Preach (USA)
	Dhaka (USA)	Icecapade (USA)
		Cloudy Day Sunny (USA)

SALES YEARLINGS OF 2018

Sold in Euros

	bc - Brick Tops (by Danehill Dancer) - Tatts IRE - September - €30,000
	bc - Delantera (by Lawman) - Arqana - August - €30,000
Owar (FR)	bc - Kointreau (by Desert King) - Arqana - August - €16,000
	bf - Solfilia (by Teofilo) - Goffs - October - €15,000
Dilligency (GB)	bc - Crystal Moments (by Haafhd) - Tatts IRE - September - €14,000
	bf - Motheeba (by Mustanfar) - Osarus - September - €9,000
	bf - Strawberry Leaf (by Unfuwain) - Goffs - November - €6,000
	bf - Free Entry (by Approve) - Arqana - August - €5,000
	bf - Frozen Princess (by Showcasing) - Tatts IRE - September - €5,000
	bf - Solfilia (by Teofilo) - Goffs - February - €5,000 (p/s)
	brc - Eve (by Rainbow Quest) - Tatts IRE - September - €3,000
	bf - Starbotton (by Kyllachy) - Goffs - February - €3,000
	bf - Kozmina Bay (by Notnowcato) - Goffs - November - €2,000
	bc - Audrey Brown (by Mind Games) - Goffs - February - €1,000 (p/s)
	bc - Audrey Brown (by Mind Games) - Goffs - November - €1,000
	bf - Serene Dream (by Oasis Dream) - Goffs - February - €1,000

Sold in Guineas

	bc - Amazed (by Clantime) - Tattersalls - October - 95,000gns
	bc - Primo Lady (by Lucky Story) - Tattersalls - October - 65,000gns

Headley George (IRE)	bc - Silent Secret (by Dubai Destination) - Tattersalls - October - 40,000gns
	bc - Frequent (by Three Valleys) - Tattersalls - October - 36,000gns
Quimerico (GB)	bc - Peyto Princess (by Bold Arrangement) - Tattersalls - October - 23,000gns
	bf - Amitola (by Choisir) - Tattersalls - October - 12,000gns
	bf - Phantom Spirit (by Invincible Spirit) - Tattersalls - October - 10,000gns
Black Morning (GB)	bf - Bright Morning (by Storm Cat) - Tattersalls - October - 8,000gns
	bc - Sugar Beet (by Beat Hollow) - Tattersalls - October - 7,000gns
	bf - Sunny York (by Vale Of York) - Tattersalls - October - 6,000gns
	bc - Her Honour (by Shamardal) - Tattersalls - October - 5,500gns
	bf - Jollification (by Acclamation) - Tattersalls - October - 5,500gns
	bf - Nolas Lolly (by Lomitas) - Tattersalls - February - 2,200gns
	bf - Chili Run (by Hurricane Run) - Tattersalls - October - 2,000gns
	bf - Three Ducks (by Diktat) - Tattersalls - October - 1,500gns
	bc - Tafawut (by Nayef) - Tattersalls - October - 1,000gns
	bc - Amber Heights (by Kyllachy) - Tattersalls - October - 800gns

Sold in Pounds

Good Time Charlie (GB)	bc - Our Faye (by College Chapel) - Goffs UK - August - £35,000
	bf - Satsuma (by Compton Place) - Goffs UK - August - £35,000
	bc - Shifting Moon (by Kheleyf) - Goffs UK - August - £35,000

Mischief Star (GB)	bc - Red Mischief (by Red Clubs) - Goffs UK - August - £30,000
Dynamighty (GB)	bf - Weisse Socken (by Acclamation) - Goffs UK - August - £22,000
Due A Win (GB)	bc - Malelane (by Prince Sabo) - Goffs UK - August - £20,000
	brc - Risk A Look (by Observatory) - Goffs UK - August - £16,000
	bc - Chicklade (by Firebreak) - Tatts IRE Ascot - September - £10,000
	bf - Nizhoni (by Mineshaft) - Goffs UK - August - £10,000
	bc - Spritzeria (by Bigstone) - Goffs UK - August - £10,000
	bf - Szabo's Art (by Excellent Art) - Goffs UK - August - £10,000
	bc - Unwrapit (by Tapit) - Goffs UK - August - £10,000
	bc - Triveni (by Lando) - Goffs UK - August - £4,000
	bc - Jules (by Danehill) - Tatts IRE Ascot - September - £3,500
	bc - Rosa Luxemburg (by Needwood Blade) - Goffs UK - August - £3,000
	bc - Midnight Pearl (by Woodman) - Goffs UK - August - £2,500

Not Sold (inc. vendor buy-backs)

bc - Ahwahnee (by Compton Place) - Tatts IRE - September

bc - Aubrietia (by Dutch Art) - Goffs UK - August

bc - Audrey Brown (by Mind Games) - Goresbridge - July

bc - Belle Of Honour (by Honour And Glory) - Tatts IRE - September

bc - Bling Bling (by Indian Ridge) - Tattersalls - November

bf - Diapsaon (by Mull Of Kintyre) - Tattersalls - October

Meliodas (GB)	bc - Dubai Legend (by Cadeaux Genereux) - Tattersalls - October
	bc - Elysee (by Fantastic Light) - Tatts IRE - September
	bf - Investiture (by Invincible Spirit) - Goffs UK - October
	bc - Lady Sledmere (by Barathea) - Tattersalls - February
	bc - M'selle (by Elnadim) - Tatts IRE Ascot - September
	bc - Miss Meticulous (by Bahamian Bounty) - Tattersalls - October
	grc - Moss Likely (by Clodovil) - Tatts IRE - September
	bf - Random (by Shamardal) - Goffs UK - August
	bf - Roodle (by Xaar) - Tattersalls - October
Ice Skate (GB)	grf - Skiing (by Sakhee's Secret) - Goffs UK - August
	bc - Small Fortune (by Anabaa) - Goffs UK - August
	bc - Sweet Alabama (by Johannesburg) - Tatts IRE - September
	bc - Think Snow (by Giant's Causeway) - Goffs - October
	bf - Yankee Belle (by Yankee Gentleman) - Tatts IRE Ascot - September

EARL OF TINSDAL (GER)

Earl Of Tinsdal (by Black Sam Bellamy) was a triple Group 1 winner over 12 furlongs, his best form came on soft and heavy ground, but he was also a pattern scorer over 10 furlongs on good. He was also multiple Group 1-placed, including when chasing home Waldpark in the Deutsches Derby and Meandre in the Grosser Preis von Berlin, and he was a dual winner over a mile as a two-year-old.

He is a son of Black Sam Bellamy (by Sadler's Wells), who spent five years at Gestut Fahrhof before moving to become a National Hunt sire at Shade Oak Stud in England where he remained until his death last year. That stallion was, of course, the Group 1-winning full-brother to Galileo and half-brother to Sea The Stars (by Cape Cross).

One of three black stakes winners out of Earthly Paradise (by Dashing Blade), Earl Of Tinsdal's dam has five blacktype siblings – including six-figure earner and Group 3 scorer Empire Storm (by Storming Home) – and his winning grandam, Emy Coasting (by El Gran Senor), is a daughter of multiple US stakes winner Coast Patrol (by Cornish Prince).

Although he may get some late-season two-year-old winners at around a mile, the best of his flat runners are likely to prove best over middle-distances and staying trips as three-year-olds and older horses. There is a good program for those divisions in Germany and France, which is where most of his offspring are likely to race. Additionally, given the profile of his sire, it can be expected that some of his progeny will also go on to do well under National Hunt rules, and that could bring him to the attention of a broader audience in Ireland and Britain.

SUMMARY DETAILS

Stood in 2016: Gestut Helenenhof, Germany
Fee in 2016: €4,000
Career highlights: 6 wins inc Rheinland-Pokal (Gr1), Gran Premio di Milano (Gr1), Gran Premio del Jockey Club (Gr1), Fruhjahrs-Rennen (Gr3), 2nd Preis Von Europa (Gr1), Grosser Preis von Berlin (Gr1), Deutsches Derby (Gr1), Preis der Sparkassen Finanzgruppe (Gr3), 3rd Grosser Preis von Bayern

(Gr1-twice), Preis von Europa (Gr1-twice), Oleander-Rennen (Gr3)
Standing in 2019: Gestut Helenenhof, Germany
Fee in 2019: €4,000
Stallions by his sire include: Earl Of Tinsdal (2yo)

EARL OF TINSDAL (GER) – bay 2008

Black Sam Bellamy (IRE)	Sadler's Wells (USA)	Northern Dancer (CAN)
		Fairy Bridge (USA)
	Urban Sea (USA)	Miswaki (USA)
		Allegretta
Earthly Paradise (GER)	Dashing Blade	Elegant Air
		Sharp Castan
	Emy Coasting (USA)	El Gran Senor (USA)
		Coast Patrol (USA)

SALES YEARLINGS OF 2018
Sold in Euros

Happy Countess (GER) brf - Humaita (by Surumu) - BBAG - October - €9,000

Verite (GER) brf - Vareze (by Duke Of Marmalade) - BBAG - October - €5,000

Bear Lake (GER) brc - Bear Diva (by Desideratum) - BBAG - October - €1,000

Not Sold

Komblume (GER) bf - Koenigin Turf (by Big Shuffle) - BBAG - October

So Early (GER) brc - So Fair (by Zinaad) - BBAG - October

EVASIVE'S FIRST (FR)

The first winner and stakes winner for the regally-related stallion Evasive (by Elusive Quality), this chestnut great-grandson of Gone West (by Mr Prospector) spent a season at Haras de Grandcamp, in France, before being exported to Tunisia. He was a listed winner over seven furlongs, his pattern success came at a mile – both as a two-year-old – and there were only seven foals in his first crop.

His dam Zalia (by Oasis Dream) is a half-sister to the pattern-placed miler Hashbrown (by Big Shuffle), and his grandam Haraplata (by Platini) is a half-sister to two blacktype earners. One of those is the ill-fated staying hurdler Acapulco (by Galileo), and the other is that one's full-sister Jane Austen who won two of her three starts for Aidan O'Brien, including a listed contest over 12 furlongs on very soft ground at Fairyhouse.

He was precocious and had the pace to win twice over five and a half furlongs in May of his two-year-old season, and his handful of offspring may yield an early juvenile winner or two, but it is likely that some of them may need more time. Indeed, it would be no surprise to see one or two of them become middle-distance horses.

SUMMARY DETAILS

Stood in 2016: Haras de Grandcamp, France
Fee in 2016: €3,000
Career highlights: 5 wins inc Prix des Chenes (Gr3), Prix des Jouvenceaux et des Jouvencelles (L)
Standing in 2019: Tunisia
Stallions by his sire include: Evasive's First (2yo)

EVASIVE'S FIRST (FR) – bay 2013

Evasive (GB)	Elusive Quality (USA)	Gone West (USA)
		Touch Of Greatness (USA)
	Canda (USA)	Storm Cat (USA)
		East Of The Moon (USA)
Zalia (FR)	Oasis Dream (GB)	Green Desert (USA)
		Hope (IRE)
	Haraplata (GER)	Platini (GER)
		Harasava (FR)

SALES YEARLINGS OF 2018

Sold in Euros

Star Drack (IRE)   chc - Amazing Beauty (by Bahamian
                          Bounty) - Osarus - September - €26,000
                          bf - Paroledefripouille (by Marchand De
                          Sable) - Arqana - November - €3,000

FOUNTAIN OF YOUTH (IRE)

The Green Desert branch of the mighty Danzig (by Northern Dancer) line is developing three splits of its own, and although the Invincible Spirit one looks strongest so far, the Oasis Dream one is showing promise. A member of the Banstead Manor Stud team, the sprint star has 17 individual Group 1 winners to his name on the track – including 2018's additions Polydream and Pretty Pollyanna – and his early stallion sons include the blacktype sires Aqlaam, Arcano, Power, and Approve.

The last of those was a Group 2 scorer on the track, as was the standout horse among the Oasis Dream stallions to date – Showcasing. That now 12-year-old Whitsbury Manor Stud resident is responsible for sprint ace Quiet Reflection and Group 1 Keeneland Phoenix Stakes winner Advertise plus 16 other group/graded winners and another 15 who have struck at least once at listed level.

The younger Oasis Dream stallions include Bearstone Stud's Fountain Of Youth who had 70 foals in his first crop. He was an odds-on winner of a five-furlong Tipperary before finishing a three-quarter-length fourth to Extortionist in the Listed Windsor Castle Stakes, earning a Timeform rating of 103p. He was then off the track for 11 months, was well-beaten in a trio of blacktype events over seven furlongs and a mile, then dropped back to the minimum trip to take the Group 3 Sapphire Stakes at the Curragh, beating old rival Extortionist by a head. He finished that year on a Timeform rating of 111.

Fountain Of Youth is a half-brother to Group 2-placed pattern winner Elarqam (by Frankel) and so is out of the dual champion and five-time Group 1 star Attraction (by Efisio). Her top-level wins came in the 1000 Guineas, Irish 1000 Guineas, Coronation Stakes, Matron Stakes and Sun Chariot Stakes, and Timeform rated her 125. She is a half-sister to Grade 3-placed Federation (by Motivator) and also to the dam of Group 2-placed listed scorer Titi Makfi (by Makfi), and she is out of Flirtation (by Pursuit Of Love), an unraced half-sister to Group 2-placed middle-distance stakes winner Carmita (by Caerleon) and also to the dam of Group 3 Polar Cup scorer You Never Know (by Diaghlyphard).

Juvenile seven-furlong Group 1 winner Lord Of Men (by Groom Dancer), Japanese champion and mile Group 1 heroine Major Emblem (by Daiwa Major), and several Argentine-bred Grade 1 winners appear under the branches of the fourth generation of the pedigree, while the fifth dam is July Cup star Lucasland (by Lucero), whose descendants also include Timeform 129-rated and classic-winning miler Sonic Lady (by Nureyev).

Fountain Of Youth looks a likely type to get some early-season juveniles but then establish himself as a source of sprinters and milers of all age groups.

SUMMARY DETAILS

Stood in 2016: Bearstone Stud, England
Fee in 2016: £5,000
Career highlights: 2 wins inc Sapphire Stakes (Gr3)
Standing in 2019: Bearstone Stud, England
Fee in 2019: £4,500
Stallions by his sire include: Captain Gerrard (Gr1), Showcasing (Gr1), Querari (Gr1), Aqlaam (Gr2), Power (Gr2), Approve (Gr3), Arcano (Gr3), Frozen Power (L), Coach House (winners), Gale Force Ten (winners), Morpheus (winners), Reply (winners), Sri Putra (winners), Fountain Of Youth (2yo), Intrinsic (2yo), Muhaarar (2yo), Charming Thought (yearlings), Free Port Lux (yearlings), De Treville (foals)

FOUNTAIN OF YOUTH (IRE) – bay 2011

Oasis Dream (GB)	Green Desert (USA)	Danzig (USA)
		Foreign Courier (USA)
	Hope (IRE)	Dancing Brave (USA)
		Bahamian
Attraction (GB)	Efisio	Formidable (USA)
		Eldoret
	Flirtation (GB)	Pursuit Of Love (GB)
		Eastern Shore

SALES YEARLINGS OF 2018

Sold in Euros
Total Perfection (IRE)   bc - Day By Day (by Kyllachy) - Tatts
                         IRE - September - €30,000
Kiss The Ladies (ITY)   bf - Period Piece (by Intikhab) - SGA -
                         September - €10,000

bc - Crystal Malt (by Intikhab) - Goffs - October - €8,000
brc - State Anthem (by Royal Applause) - Goffs - October - €7,500
bc - Harryana To (by Compton Place) - Goffs - February - €5,500 (p/s)
bc - Say A Prayer (by Indesatchel) - Tatts IRE - September - €5,500 (p/s)

Sold in Guineas

Gift of Youth (GB)   bc - Margrets Gift (by Major Cadeaux) - Tattersalls - October - 40,000gns

Trevie Fountain (GB)   bc - Fantacise (by Pivotal) - Tattersalls - October - 28,000gns

Kokura (GB)   bc - Some Diva (by Dr Fong) - Tattersalls - October - 20,000gns
bc - Hip Flask (by Motivator) - Tattersalls - October - 18,000gns

Itwouldberudenotto (GB)   bc - Jive (by Major Cadeaux) - Tattersalls - October - 16,000gns
bf - Cadeaux Power (by Major Cadeaux) - Tattersalls - October - 15,000gns
bf - Citron (by Reel Buddy) - Tattersalls - October - 10,000gns

Expressions (GB)   bf - Punchie (by Lucky Story) - Tattersalls - October - 5,000gns
bc - Rememberance Day (by Major Cadeaux) - Tattersalls - October - 5,000gns
bf - Island Rhapsody (by Bahamian Bounty) - Tattersalls - October - 4,500gns
bc - Symphonic Dancer (by Smart Strike) - Tattersalls - October - 3,000gns
bf - Amouage Royale (by Mr Greeley) - Tattersalls - October - 1,000gns
bf - Bombalarina (by Barathea) - Tattersalls - October - 800gns
bf - Quiet Elegance (by Fantastic Light) - Tattersalls - October - 800gns

Sold in Pounds

Mahala Bay (GB)	bc - Catmint (by Piccolo) - Goffs UK - August - £50,000
	bc - Choisette (by Choisir) - Goffs UK - August - £35,000
	bf - Wether Girl (by Major Cadeaux) - Goffs UK - August - £32,000
Three Coins (GB)	bf - Bereka (by Firebreak) - Goffs UK - August - £25,000
Rajan (GB)	bc - Dayville (by Dayjur) - Goffs UK - August - £26,000
Moonlight Shadow (GB)	grc - Lone Angel (by Dark Angel) - Goffs UK - August - £24,000
Golden Fountain (IRE)	bc - Art Of Gold (by Excellent Art) - Goffs UK - August - £18,000 (p/s)
Lucas (GB)	bc - Ice Mayden (by Major Cadeaux) - Goffs UK - August - £18,000
Orlagh (GB)	bf - Big Sky (by Fastnet Rock) - Tatts IRE Ascot - September - £15,000
	bc - Harryana To (by Compton Place) - Goffs UK - August - £15,000
	bc - Miss Lesley (by Needwood Blade) - Goffs UK - December - £15,000
Jacks Black (GB)	brc - Sukuma (by Highest Honor) - Goffs UK - August - £12,000
	bc - Cards (by Tobougg) - Goffs UK - August - £10,000
Chardoneigh (GB)	bf - Razzle (by Green Desert) - Goffs UK - August - £9,000
	bf - Irrational (by Kyllachy) - Goffs UK - August - £6,000
	brc - Charcoal (by Primo Valentino) - Tatts IRE Ascot - September - £5,000
	bf - Virtuality (by Elusive Quality) - Goffs UK - October - £5,000
	bf - Find The Answer (by Vital Equine) - Goffs UK - October - £2,000
	bc - Equinox (by Medicean) - Goffs UK - October - £800

Not Sold (inc. vendor buy-backs)

	bf - Albertine Rose (by Namid) - Goffs UK - October
	bf - Bravo (by Indian Charlie) - Goffs UK - October
	bc - Clodianna (by Clodovil) - Goffs UK - October
	bf - Kyllarney (by Kyllachy) - Goffs UK - August
	bf - La Zamora (by Lujain) - Goffs UK - October
	bc - Mad Annie (by Anabaa) - Goffs UK - August
Elixir Sky (GB)	bf - Millinsky (by Stravinsky) - Tattersalls - October
Ebony Adams (GB)	bf - Mortitia (by Dansili) - Tattersalls - October
	bc - Nellie Ellis (by Compton Place) - Tatts IRE - September
	bf - So Discreet (by Tragic Role) - Goffs UK - October

FRESHMAN SIRES OF 2019

FREE EAGLE (IRE)

With 22 Group 1 winners among a current total of 127 blacktype scorers, dual Derby and dual Breeders' Cup hero High Chaparral is among the most successful stallion sons of the great Sadler's Wells (by Northern Dancer). Sadly, like Montjeu, he died in his teens. It is early yet for his handful of stallion sons, although the signs are encouraging. So You Think has five southern hemisphere Group 1 winners to date, Dundeel has a top-level winner in each of his first two crops, and Toronado made a promising start with his first juveniles in 2018, his double-digit tally including five colts who earned a blacktype placing. The Irish National Stud-based Free Eagle is a freshman sire of 2019, his initial yearlings found buyers at all levels of the market and a few of them making a six-figure sum.

Such was the impression that this former Dermot Weld-trained horse made when thrashing Orchestra by five and a half lengths in a mile maiden in August of his juvenile year that he was a 2/5 favourite to beat Australia in a Group 3 contest over the same course and distance the following month, and widely regarded as a major Derby contender for 2014. As is widely known, Australia beat him by six lengths that day, and while that chestnut went on to add the Derby, Irish Derby and Juddmonte International Stakes the following year, Free Eagle missed a full 12 months off the track before returning to action with a pair of efforts that saw him earn a Timeform rating of 128p.

First, he beat Elleval by seven lengths in the Group 3 Kilternan Stakes over 10 furlongs on fast ground at Leopardstown and then chased home Noble Mission and Al Kazeem on heavy ground in the Group 1 Champion Stakes at Ascot. His final two outings at four were disappointing, but he started that year by short-heading The Grey Gatsby in the Group 1 Prince of Wales's Stakes at Ascot and taking third to Golden Horn and Found in the Group 1 Irish Champion Stakes at Leopardstown, beaten by a length and half a length. Timeform kept him on a mark of 128.

Free Eagle is a half-brother to the multiple Group 2 winner Custom Cut (by Notnowcato) – who is effective at around a mile – and also to Sapphire (by Medicean), who won the Group 2 Qipco British Champions Fillies and Mares Stakes and filled the runners-up spot in the Group 1 Pretty Polly Stakes. Their dam, Polished Gem (by Danehill), is a winning full-sister to Grade 1 Matriarch Stakes heroine Dress To Thrill and so a daughter of Group 1 Irish 1000 Guineas winner Trusted Partner (by Affirmed). That classic scorer – whose descendants also include Group 1 Criterium International victor Vert De Grece (by Verglas) – is a full-sister to three stakes winners and out of US juvenile filly champion Talking Picture (by Speak John).

Those siblings include Group 2 scorer Easy To Copy whose descendants include the Group 1 Grand Prix de Paris and Group 1 Sydney Cup winner Gallante (by Montjeu) and dual US Grade 2 winner Amira's Prince (by Teofilo), who is a US-based freshman sire. They also include the pattern-placed stakes winner Epicure's Garden who became the dam of the Group 2 Blandford Stakes and dual US Grade 2 heroine Lisieux Rose (by Generous) and grandam of the Group 1-placed, Group 2-winning stayer Forgotten Rules (by Nayef).

This pedigree is that of a top-class racehorse and makes Free Eagle an interesting stallion prospect. There were 80 foals in his first crop, and although some will win as two-year-olds, that is likely to be mostly in the second half of the season. In the long term, he looks likely to get his best winners in the broad seven-to-14-furlong range, with the chance that a few will become Cup horses.

SUMMARY DETAILS

Stood in 2016: Irish National Stud, Ireland
Fee in 2016: €20,000
Career highlights: 3 wins inc Prince of Wales's Stakes (Gr1), Kilternan Stakes (Gr3), Juvenile Turf Trial Golden Fleece Stakes (Gr3), 3rd Irish Champion Stakes (Gr1), Champion Stakes (Gr1)
Standing in 2019: Irish National Stud, Ireland
Fee in 2019: €12,500
Stallions by his sire include: Dundeel (Gr1), So You Think (Gr1), Redwood (Gr3), Tai Chi (Gr3), Lord Chaparral (winners), Magadan (winners), Toronado (winners), Wrote (winners), Contributor (2yo), Free Eagle (2yo), Alpine Eagle (yearlings), Karaktar (yearlings), Tivaci (yearlings)

FREE EAGLE (IRE) – bay 2011

High Chaparral (IRE)	Sadler's Wells (USA)	Northern Dancer (CAN)
		Fairy Bridge (USA)
	Kasora (IRE)	Darshaan
		Kozana
Polished Gem (IRE)	Danehill (USA)	Danzig (USA)
		Razyana (USA)
	Trusted Partner (USA)	Affirmed (USA)
		Talking Picture (USA)

SALES YEARLINGS OF 2018

Sales in Euros

Al Qaasim (IRE)	bc - Nebraas (by Green Desert) - Goffs - October - €400,000
	bf - Serisia (by Exit To Nowhere) - Arqana - August - €200,000
Auxilia (IRE)	bf - Ispa Loquitur (by Unfuwain) - Goffs - October - €140,000
	chc - Badr Al Badoor (by Acclamation) - Goffs - October - €90,000
Alpin King (IRE)	bc - Rosa's Cantina (by Paco Boy) - Goffs - October - €75,000
Justifier (IRE)	chc - Pale Orchid (by Invincible Spirit) - Goffs - October - €60,000
Swooping Eagle (IRE)	bc - Weekend Lady (by Bahamian Bounty) - Goffs - October - €60,000
	bc - Ohio (by Teofilo) - Tatts IRE - September - €40,000
	bc - Spinamix (by Linamix) - Goffs - October - €40,000
Khalifa Sat (IRE)	bc - Thermopylae (by Tenby) - Goffs - October - €40,000
	bc - Princess Savoie (by Tamayuz) - Tatts IRE - September - €30,000
	bc - Classic Remark (by Dr Fong) - Goffs - October - €25,000 (p/s)
	bc - Dulcian (by Shamardal) - Goffs - October - €25,000
	bc - Cland Di San Jore (by Lando) - Tatts IRE - September - €21,000

bc - Peace Signal (by Time For A Change) - Tatts IRE - September - €21,000

bf - Chanter (by Lomitas) - Goffs - October - €16,000

bf - Keilogue (by Invincible Spirit) - Arqana - August - €15,000

bc - Marque Royale (by Royal Academy) - Tatts IRE - September - €13,000

bc - Ohio (by Teofilo) - Goffs - February - €11,000

bf - Burma Star (by Shamardal) - Goffs - November - €10,000

bf - Gelenschik (by Dalakhani) - Tatts IRE - September - €9,500

bf - Legs Lawlor (by Unbridled) - Tatts IRE - September - €9,000

bc - Champagne Mistress (by Kyllachy) - Goffs - October - €7,000

chf - Perivale (by Street Cry) - Goffs - November - €6,500 (p/s)

bc - Jolie Etoile (by Diesis) - Goffs - October - €6,000

bf - Afilla (by Dansili) - Goffs - October - €5,000

chf - Perivale (by Street Cry) - Goffs - February - €5,000

grf - Glassathura (by Verglas) - Tatts IRE - September - €4,000

brf - Wild Step (by Footstepsinthesand) - Goffs - October - €4,000

bf - Pavlopetri (by Danehill Dancer) - Goffs - November - €1,000

Sold in Guineas

bf - Malaspina (by Whipper) - Tattersalls - October - 250,000gns

Free Falcon (IRE)   bc - Regalline (by Green Desert) - Tattersalls - October - 150,000gns

FREE EAGLE (IRE)

	bc - Bryanstown (by Galileo) - Tattersalls - November - 72,000gns
Prinec of Eagles (IRE)	bc - Sleeping Beauty (by Oasis Dream) - Tattersalls - October - 70,000gns
Big Wing (IRE)	b/brc - Orafinitis (by Oratorio) - Tattersalls - October - 60,000gns
	bc - Shauna's Princess (by Soviet Star) - Tattersalls - October - 50,000gns
	chf - Super Saturday (by Pivotal) - Tattersalls - October - 40,000gns
Proclaimer (GB)	bc - Pious (by Bishop Of Cashel) - Tattersalls - October - 36,000gns
	bc - Carmens Fate (by Cape Cross) - Tattersalls - October - 32,000gns
	bf - Indian Maiden (by Indian Ridge) - Tattersalls - October - 30,000gns
	bf - Dundel's Spirit (by Invincible Spirit) - Tattersalls - November - 20,000gns
	bf - Penny Rose (by Danehill Dancer) - Tattersalls - October - 8,000gns (p/s)
	bf - Alayna (by Cape Cross) - Tattersalls - October - 1,000gns

Not Sold (inc. vendor buy-backs)

	brf - Acquifer (by Oasis Dream) - Tattersalls - October
	chc - Best Be Careful (by Exceed And Excel) - Tatts IRE - September
Sparrow Hawk (GB)	bf - Calico Moon (by Seeking The Gold) - Tatts IRE Ascot - September
	bc - Capsaicin (by Invincible Spirit) - Goffs - November
	bf - Curious Lashes (by Footstepsinthesand) - Tatts IRE - September
	chf - Fafinta (by Indian Ridge) - SGA - September
	bc - Meet Marhaba (by Marju) - Tattersalls - October

Uncle Sid (GB)

bf - Nitya (by Indian Ridge) - Tatts IRE
- September
bc - Paisley (by Pivotal) - Tattersalls -
October
bf - Pesse (by Eagle Eyed) - Tattersalls -
October
bf - Poplar Close (by Canford Cliffs) -
Goffs - October
bc - Quixotic (by Pivotal) - Goffs -
October
bf - Reveal The Star (by Aptitude) -
Goffs - October
bf - Traveller's Tales (by Cape Cross) -
Tatts IRE - September
chc - Uvinza (by Bertolini) - Tattersalls -
October
bf - Velvet Star (by Galileo) - Tattersalls
- October
bf - Wandering Star (by Verglas) -
Baden-Baden - August

FREE EAGLE (IRE)

FRENCH NAVY (GB)

By the sire of notable international sire Lope De Vega (by Shamardal), Kildangan Stud's French Navy has the unusual distinction of having been a stakes winner every year from two to seven years of age. He is also from a family that has previously yielded a champion sire. There were only 42 foals in his first crop – at one time a full book but, in recent decades, on the small side – and he is a horse who could spring a few surprises. He was best from eight to 10 furlongs, was a mile pattern winner at two, and looks likely to get his best results from those competing in the broad seven-to-14-furlong range.

He is a half-brother to the high-class dual-purpose gelding Sea Lord (by Cape Cross), and his dam – the French 10-furlong listed scorer First Fleet (by Woodman) – is out of a half-sister to several horses of note, one of whom is the stakes winner and multiple Indian champion sire Razeen (by Northern Dancer). King George-third Assatis (by Topsider) was a Group 1 winner in Italy, Warrshan (by Northern Dancer) won the Group 3 Gordon Stakes and finished third in the Group 2 Great Voltigeur Stakes, and Hidden Dreams (by Soviet Star), who did her part for the family at stud, became the dam of a Grade 1-placed dual Grade 3 winner in South America.

Their dam, the unraced Secret Asset (by Graustark), was out of the US juvenile filly champion Numbered Account (by Buckpasser), which made her a half-sister to Grade 1 star and leading sire Private Account (by Damascus), to stakes-placed runner and notable sire Polish Numbers (by Danzig), and to Grade 1 heroine and influential broodmare Dance Number (by Northern Dancer). Her offspring featured juvenile champion, Grade 1 Travers Stakes winner and successful sire Rhythm (by Mr Prospector), and her descendants include the Grade 1 winners Frost Giant (by Giant's Causeway), Girolamo (by A.P. Indy), Got Lucky (by A.P. Indy), Imagining (by Giant's Causeway), and Super Saver (by Maria's Mon). The latter's early offspring include Grade 1 stars Runhappy, Embellish The Lace, and Competitive Edge, the latter also now a US-based freshman sire.

It should also be noted that Numbered Account's full-sister Playmate was the dam of dual Irish Group 3 scorer and leading international sire Woodman (by Mr Prospector), which makes

French Navy inbred 4x5 to those mares' parents, Buckpasser (by Tom Fool) and Intriguing (by Swaps). He is also inbred 4x3 to Mr Prospector (by Raise a Native) and 5x4 to Northern Dancer (by Nearctic). There is no doubt that French Navy has a pedigree that gives him a chance of siring some high-class offspring.

SUMMARY DETAILS

Stood in 2016: Kildangan Stud, Ireland

Fee in 2016: €4,000

Career highlights: 11 wins inc Diomed Stakes (Gr3), Earl of Sefton Stakes (Gr3), Select Stakes (Gr3), Prix de Chenes (Gr3), Festival Stakes (L), Ben Marshall Stakes (L-twice), Midsummer Stakes (L), 2nd Earl of Sefton Stakes (Gr3), Steventon Stakes (L), Ben Marshall Stakes (L), 3rd Paradise Stakes (L)

Standing in 2019: Kildangan Stud, Ireland

Fee in 2019: €4,000

Stallions by his sire include: Captain Sonador (Gr1), Lope De Vega (Gr1), Casamento (Gr2), Mukhadram (Gr3), Shamoline Warrior (L), Ghibellines (winners), Gingerbread Man (winners), Shakespearean (winners), Sommerabend (winners), Amaron (2yo), Crackerjack King (2yo), French Navy (2yo), Zazou (2yo), Bow Creek (yearlings), Dariyan (yearlings), Lightning Moon (yearlings), Balios (foals), Doha Dream (new)

FRENCH NAVY (GB) – bay 2008

			Storm Cat (USA)
Shamardal (USA)	Giant's Causeway (USA)		Mariah's Storm (USA)
	Helsinki (GB)		Machiavellian (USA)
			Helen Street
First Fleet (USA)	Woodman (USA)		Mr Prospector (USA)
			Playmate (USA)
	Frankova (USA)		Nureyev (USA)
			Secret Asset (USA)

SALES YEARLINGS OF 2018

Sold in Euros

Score (IRE)　　　　　　　bc - Love Match (by Danehill Dancer) - Goffs - November - €23,000
bf - Verba's Best (by King's Best) - Arqana - October - €12,000

bc - Deceptive (by Red Ransom) - Goffs - February - €9,500
bc - Hannah's Magic (by Lomitas) - Goffs - October - €8,000
bc - Invincible Wings (by Invincible Spirit) - Goffs - November - €8,000 (p/s)
bc - Take A Rest (by Dylan Thomas) - Tatts IRE - September - €6,200
bc - Scala Romana (by Holy Roman Emperor) - Tatts IRE - September - €4,000
grc - Tuilelaith (by Clodovil) - Goffs - November - €2,800
bc - Divas Dream (by Refuse To Bend) - Goffs - November - €1,500
bc - Glasnas Giant (by Giant's Causeway) - Goffs - November - €1,000
bf - Intimate Secret (by Invincible Spirit) - Goffs - November - €1,000

Sold in Guineas

bc - Ouija's Sister (by Groom Dancer) - Tattersalls - November - 5,500gns
b/brc - Quail Landing (by Mark Of Esteem) - Tattersalls - October - 5,000gns
bc - Gipsy Doll (by Dansili) - Tattersalls - October - 2,000gns

Sold in Pounds

Paddy Elliott (IRE)

bc - Siphon Melody (by Siphon) - Goffs UK - August - £9,000
bc - Maraglen (by Rock Of Gibraltar) - Goffs UK - August - £2,000
bf - Square Pants (by King Of Kings) - Goffs UK - October - £800
bf - Kathy's Rocket (by Gold Legend) - Tatts IRE Ascot - December - £600

FRENCH NAVY (GB)

Not Sold (inc. vendor buy-backs)

Sophar Sogood (IRE)   bc - Cloud Break (by Dansili) - Goffs - November

bc - D'Addario (by Galileo) - Goffs - November

chf - Ellen's Girl (by Desert Prince) - Goffs - November

bc - Korresia (by Elnadim) - Tatts IRE - September

bc - Lucky Flirt (by Gulch) - Tatts IRE - September

bc - Magadar (by Lujain) - Tatts IRE - September

bc - Main Opinion (by Ivan Denisovich) - Goffs - November

bf - Mikes Baby (by Key Of Luck) - Goffs - November

chc - Primaprima (by More Than Ready) - Arqana - August

bf - Tallawalla (by Oratorio) - Goffs - November

FULBRIGHT (GB)

Fulbright (by Exceed And Excel) is by the sire of Group 1-siring stallions Excelebration, Helmet, and Sidestep, he was a six-furlong stakes winner at two, won the Group 2 Challenge Stakes over seven furlongs at Newmarket at three, was Group 2-placed at a mile, and he is a Kildangan Stud resident who has 35 representatives in his first crop.

He is the best of nine winners out one-time scorer Lindfield Belle (by Fairy King), and those siblings include Group 3 Prix Eclipse winner Domingues (by Danetime) and Group 2-placed, dual stakes-winning sprinter and blacktype sire Baltic King (by Danetime). Their grandam, Tecmessa (by Home Guard), was an unraced full-sister to Group 3 Prix du Petit Couvert winner and Group 1 Prix Jacques le Marois third Manjam, and those are the highlights of the first four generations of the pedigree.

Fulbright looks likely to get winners at all ages, with candidates for some of the lucrative sales races plus sprint, mile and 10-furlong handicaps among them, and potentially the occasional blacktype horse.

SUMMARY DETAILS

Stood in 2016: Kildangan Stud, Ireland
Fee in 2016: €4,000
Career highlights: 9 wins inc Challenge Stakes (Gr2), Fortune Stakes (L), Woodcote Stakes (L), 2nd Firebreak Stakes (Gr3), Superior Mile (L), 3rd Al Maktoum Challenge Round 1 (Gr2), Zabeel Mile (Gr2)
Standing in 2019: Kildangan Stud, Ireland
Fee in 2019: €4,000
Stallions by his sire include: Excelebration (Gr1), Helmet (Gr1), Sidestep (Gr1), Bungle Inthejungle (Gr3), Exceedingly Good (Gr3), Burwaaz (winners), Kuroshio (winners), Fulbright (2yo), Outstrip (2yo), Buratino (yearlings), Cotai Glory (foals), James Garfield (new)

FULBRIGHT (GB) – bay 2009

Exceed And Excel (AUS)	Danehill (USA)	Danzig (USA)
		Razyana (USA)
	Patrona (USA)	Lomond (USA)
		Gladiolus (USA)
Lindfield Belle (IRE)	Fairy King (USA)	Northern Dancer (CAN)
		Fairy Bridge (USA)
	Tecmessa	Home Guard (USA)
		Two Fast

SALES YEARLINGS OF 2018

Sold in Euros

bc - Baileys Forever (by Mount Nelson) - Goffs - February - €19,000
bc - Letizia Sophia (by Shamardal) - Tatts IRE - September - €11,000
bc - Church Road (by Danehill Dancer) - Goffs - February - €8,000
bf - Heavenly River (by Stormy River) - Tatts IRE - September - €8,000
bf - Nouvelle Nova (by Noverre) - Goffs - November - €3,800
bf - Nan Power (by Iffraaj) - Goffs - October - €3,000
bf - Pinewoods Lily (by Indian Ridge) - Goffs - November - €2,000
bf - Girl Ranger (by Bushranger) - Goffs - November - €1,200
bf - Beauty And Style (by King Of Kings) - Tatts IRE - September - €1,000 (p/s)

Sold in Guineas
Winterburn (IRE)

bg - Kotdiji (by Mtoto) - Tattersalls - November - 20,000gns
bf - Music Pearl (by Oratorio) - Tattersalls - October - 3,500gns

Sold in Pounds
Richard Rhb (IRE)

bc - Royal Interlude (by King's Theatre) - Goffs UK - August - £22,000

Various (IRE)   bc - Miss Frangipane (by Acclamation) -
Goffs UK - August - £16,000
bf - With Colour (by Rainbow Quest) -
Tatts IRE Ascot - September - £6,500

Not Sold (inc. vendor buy-backs)

bc - Ashdali (by Grand Lodge) - Tatts
IRE - September
bc - Baileys Forever (by Mount Nelson)
- Goffs UK - August
bc - Church Road (by Danehill Dancer)
- Goffs - November
bc - Firecross (by Pivotal) - Goffs -
November
bf - Handsinthemist (by Lend A Hand)
- Tatts IRE - November
bc - Mary Sea (by Selkirk) - Tatts IRE -
September
bc - Midris (by Namid) - Goffs -
November
bc - Smilelikeyoumeanit (by Authorized)
- Tatts IRE - September

G FORCE (IRE)

G Force is one of three Group 1 winners by the top-level-winning miler Tamayuz (by Nayef), and that stallion's 21 blacktype scorers also include the juvenile Group 2 winner and successful young sire Sir Prancealot who, like G Force, began his stud career at Tally-Ho Stud. That horse is now in Australia, and his first crop – now four-year-olds – features the Group/Grade 2 winners Beau Recall, Sir Dancealot, and Madam Dancealot. The latter was a nose second in the Grade 1 Gamely Stakes at Santa Anita last year, whereas 2018's Group 2 Hungerford Stakes and Group 2 Lennox Stakes hero Sir Dancealot was fourth in the Group 1 July Cup.

Sadly, the odds of G Force making a similar impact are small, however, as he proved to be subfertile, fathered just eight foals, was gelded and returned to training. He was a member of the David O'Meara team when landing the Group 1 Sprint Cup at Haydock back in 2014, he was a stakes-placed spring winner last year for Adrian Keatley, and was last seen in action when finishing down the field in the Ayr Gold Cup in September. At his peak, Timeform rated him 126.

G Force is a half-brother to the 10-furlong listed scorer Laajooj (by Azamour) and Grade 3 Miesque Stakes winner Louvain (by Sinndar). The latter is also notable as being the dam of Flotilla (by Mizzen Mast), the Grade 1 Breeders' Cup Juvenile Fillies Turf heroine of 2012 who went on to take the following year's Group 1 Poule d'Essai des Pouliches (French 1000 Guineas). Their dam, Flanders (by Common Grounds), won the Listed Scarborough Stakes, was runner-up in the Group 2 King's Stand Stakes and third in the Group 2 Lowther Stakes, and her siblings include Ascot Family (by Desert Style), the stakes-winning dam of Group 2 Prix Robert Papin winner and Group 1 Prix Morny runner-up Family One (by Dubai Destination).

Flanders is also a half-sister to Capulet Monteque (by Camacho), who is the dam of Group 2 Rockfel Stakes winner Juliet Capulet (by Dark Angel), and to Land Army (by Desert Style), the unraced dam of Lethal Force (by Dark Angel). That Timeform 128-rated grey landed both the Group 1 Diamond Jubilee Stakes and Group 1 July Cup, stands at Cheveley Park Stud, and has several blacktype horses to his name so far.

G Force's handful of progeny include some well-related individuals, and it would be no surprise to see them so well in sprints or over a mile. It remains to be seen if any of them can prove to be as talented a racehorse as he was.

SUMMARY DETAILS
Stood in 2016: Tally-Ho Stud, Ireland
Fee in 2016: €8,000
Career highlights: 4 wins inc Sprint Cup (Gr1), 2nd City Walls Stakes (L), 3rd Cork Stakes (L), Scurry Stakes (L)
Standing in 2019: withdrawn from stud in 2016
Stallions by his sire include: Sir Prancealot (Gr2), G Force (2yo)

G FORCE (IRE) – bay 2009

Tamayuz (GB)	Nayef (USA)	Gulch (USA)
		Height Of Fashion (FR)
	Al Ishq (FR)	Nureyev (USA)
		Allez Les Trois (USA)
Flanders (IRE)	Common Grounds	Kris
		Sweetly (FR)
	Family At War (USA)	Exploded (USA)
		Sometimes Perfect (USA)

SALES YEARLINGS OF 2018
Sold in Guineas
Centrifuge (IRE)   Bf - Of Course Darling (by Dalakhani) - Tattersalls - October - 800gns

Sold in Pounds
Out of Here (IRE)   Chc - Wee Jean (by Captain Gerrard) - Goffs UK - August - £35,000
Typhoon Lily (IRE)   Chf - Rise Up Lotus (by Zebedee) - Goffs UK - August - £32,000
Bc - Beauty Of The Sea (by Elusive Quality) - Goffs UK - August - £27,000
Contract Kid (IRE)   Grc - Danamight (by Danetime) - Goffs UK - August - £18,000
Bc - Chizzler (by Baltic King) - Tatts IRE Ascot - September - £13,000

G FORCE (IRE)

Bf - Amalfi (by Acclamation) - Tatts
IRE Ascot - September - £4,500

Not Sold (inc. vendor buy-backs)
Bf - Edmondstown Lass (by Imperial
Ballet) - Goffs - November

GALIWAY (GB)

Prolific champion sire Galileo (by Sadler's Wells) is well established as a leading sire of sires, and his growing list of sons of stud includes Galiway, a pattern-placed stakes winner who won two of his five starts. He is bred on the popular Galileo – Danehill (by Danzig) cross, stands at Haras de Colleville and has 31 registered members in his first crop.

He is out of the Group 3 Prix Perth winner and Group 2 Prix d'Astarte runner-up Danzigaway, which makes him a half-brother to Grade 1 Breeders' Cup Mile third, dual US Grade 2 scorer, and successful blacktype sire Silent Name (by Sunday Silence). Their unraced half-sister Zigarra (by Halling) is the dam of the pattern-placed triple listed scorer Battalion (by Authorized), whereas their dam's siblings feature Gold Away (by Goldneyev). He got his best win in the Group 2 Prix du Muguet, he was placed in each of the Prix Jean Prat, Prix Maurice de Gheest, Prix d'Ispahan, and two editions of the Prix du Moulin de Longchamp – all Group 1 – and the standout among his offspring, by a long way, is the multiple Group 1 star Alexander Goldrun.

Danzigaway's siblings also include the Group 3 Prix du Calvados winner Blushing Gleam (by Caerleon) and a mare called Lishaway (by Polish Precedent), the dam of Group 3 Solario Stakes scorer Foss Way (by Desert Prince). Therefore, Galiway's grandam is the stakes-placed Blushing Away (by Blushing Groom), and his third dam is the Grade 1-placed, Grade 2 Alcibiades Stakes heroine Sweet Revenge (by Raja Baba). Both his fourth and fifth dams – Away (by Blue Prince) and Golly (by Alorter) – were also stakes winners. He may get some two-year-old winners in the second half of the season, and his offspring look likely to prove best in the broad seven-to-14-furlong range, with some of them potentially staying a bit farther.

SUMMARY DETAILS

Stood in 2016: Haras de Colleville, France
Fee in 2016: €3,000
Career highlights: 2 wins inc Prix Le Fabuleux (L), 2nd Horris Hill Stakes (Gr3), 3rd Prix de Fontainebleau (Gr3)
Standing in 2019: Haras de Colleville, France
Fee in 2019: €3,000

GALIWAY (GB)

Stallions by his sire include: Cima De Triomphe (Gr1), Frankel (Gr1), Heliostatic (Gr1), Intello (Gr1), Nathaniel (Gr1), New Approach (Gr1), Rip Van Winkle (Gr1), Roderic O'Connor (Gr1), Ruler Of The World (Gr1), Sixties Icon (Gr1), Soldier Of Fortune (Gr1), Teofilo (Gr1), Treasure Beach (Gr1)

GALIWAY (GB) – bay 2011

Galileo (IRE)	Sadler's Wells (USA)	Northern Dancer (CAN)
		Fairy Bridge (USA)
	Urban Sea (USA)	Miswaki (USA)
		Allegretta
Danzigaway (USA)	Danehill (USA)	Danzig (USA)
		Razyana (USA)
	Blushing Away (USA)	Blushing Groom (FR)
		Sweet Revenge (USA)

SALES YEARLINGS OF 2018

Sold in Euros

Kenway (FR)	chc - Kendam (by Kendargent) - Arqana - August - €56,000
Galispeed (FR)	bc - Becquaspeed (by Country Reel) - Osarus - September - €30,000
Ocean Slew (FR)	bc - Atlantic Slew (by Helissio) - Arqana - August - €27,000
Flyingbeauty (FR)	bf - Kiyrna (by Manduro) - Arqana - August - €20,000
Becquathunder (FR)	chc - Khayriya (by Valanour) - Arqana - February - €3,000
Heniway (FR)	bf - Lorenzia (by Poliglote) - Arqana - November - €1,500

Not Sold (inc. vendor buy-backs)

Galinelson (FR)	bc - Brenda Nelson (by Mount Nelson) - Osarus - September

GATEWOOD (GB)

Sadler's Wells (by Northern Dancer) had a profound influence on the breed, both in the global flat sector and in the National Hunt division, and one of the first things to catch the eye concerning Gatewood's pedigree is that he is inbred 2x3 to the great white-faced bay. The son of prolific champion sire Galileo (by Sadler's Wells) is out of Group 3 Golden Daffodil Stakes winner Felicity (by Selkirk), and his grandam is Group 1 Oaks d'Italia third Las Flores (by Sadler's Wells).

He was a 116 Timeform-rated middle-distance horse, his dam is a half-sister to the seven-furlong Group 2 winner and blacktype sire Sleeping Indian (by Indian Ridge) and full-sister to middle-distance Group 2 scorer and young Anngrove Stud stallion Aiken (by Selkirk), and his grandam is also a half-sister to two horses of note.

Dancing Goddess (by Nijinsky) won a listed sprint in Ireland, chased home Trusted Partner in the Group 1 Irish 1000 Guineas, and became the grandam of the classic-placed multiple Japanese Group 2 scorer Air Eminem (by Danehill) – the sire of blacktype-winning French hurdler Hurkhan. Bach (by Caerleon), on the other hand, won the Group 2 Royal Whip Stakes and four listed contests, he chased home Rebelline in the Group 1 Tattersalls Gold Cup and Suances in the Group 1 Prix Jean Prat, and finished third in the Grade 1 Breeders' Cup Mile, Group 1 Irish Champion Stakes, and Group 1 Coral-Eclipse Stakes before going on to a somewhat successful career as a National Hunt stallion.

All of this makes Windmill View Stud stallion Gatewood an interesting prospect, and although there are only 19 members of his first crop, it would be no surprise to see some of them prove quite smart in point-to-points, over hurdles, and fences.

SUMMARY DETAILS

Stood in 2016: Windmill View Stud, Ireland
Fee in 2016: €1,500
Career highlights: 8 wins inc Geelong Cup (Gr3), Prix de Reux (Gr3), Tapster Stakes (L), Buckhounds Stakes (L), Wolferton Handicap (L), 2nd Grand Prix de Deauville (Gr2-twice), Fred Archer Stakes (L), Quebec Stakes (L), Floodlit Stakes (L), 3rd

Cumberland Lodge Stakes (Gr3), Glorious Stakes (Gr3), Fred
Archer Stakes (L)
Standing in 2019: Windmill View Stud, Ireland
Fee in 2019: €2,000
Stallions by his sire include: Cima De Triomphe (Gr1), Frankel
(Gr1), Heliostatic (Gr1), Intello (Gr1), Nathaniel (Gr1), New
Approach (Gr1), Rip Van Winkle (Gr1), Roderic O'Connor
(Gr1), Ruler Of The World (Gr1), Sixties Icon (Gr1), Soldier Of
Fortune (Gr1), Teofilo (Gr1), Treasure Beach (Gr1)

GATEWOOD (GB) – bay 2008

Galileo (IRE)	**Sadler's Wells (USA)**	Northern Dancer (CAN)
		Fairy Bridge (USA)
	Urban Sea (USA)	Miswaki (USA)
		Allegretta
Felicity (IRE)	Selkirk (USA)	Sharpen Up
		Annie Edge
	Las Flores (IRE)	**Sadler's Wells (USA)**
		Producer (USA)

SALES YEARLINGS OF 2018

Sold in Euros

Bc - Capelvenere (by Barathea) - Tatts
IRE - February - €7,500
Bc - Lodge Princess (by Dr Massini) -
Tatts IRE - February - €4,000
Bf - Creaking Step (by Shernazar) -
Tatts IRE - November - €800

Not Sold

Bg - Madame Von Meck (by Soviet
Star) - Tatts IRE - November
Brc - Tikkanese (by Tikkanen) - Tatts
IRE - February

GLENEAGLES (IRE)

There are no guarantees in life, but it will be quite a shock if Coolmore Stud's Gleneagles fails to become a sire of Group 1 winners. It remains to be seen whether or not they will be significant horses among a long list of stakes and pattern winners, or just the occasional ones dotted throughout his career, but as a top-class son of Galileo (by Sadler's Wells) who is out of a 'blue hen' full-sister to multiple US champion sire Giant's Causeway (by Storm Cat), one could justifiably ask 'how could he fail?'

Gleneagles never ran over less than seven furlongs, and his maiden success came on his second attempt, but then he swept the Group 3 Tyros Stakes, Group 2 Futurity Stakes and Group 1 Goffs Vincent O'Brien National Stakes before passing the post a half-length and short-neck in front of Full Mast and Territories in the Group 1 Prix Jean-Luc Lagardère at Longchamp only to lose the race in the stewards' room. He beat Territories again, this time by two and a quarter lengths, when making his seasonal debut in the Group 1 2000 Guineas at Newmarket the following May, added the Group 1 Irish 2000 Guineas at the Curragh, and then justified odds-on again with a two-and-a-half-length score in the Group 1 St James's Palace Stakes at Royal Ascot.

With a clear preference for fast ground, he bypassed several potential targets but took his chance on good-to-soft at Ascot in mid-October as a prep for a shot at the Grade 1 Breeders' Cup Classic at Keeneland. Sadly, neither worked out. He was a three-length sixth in the former and then trailed home in rear behind American Pharoah, neither performance any reflection on his ability. Gleneagles was Timeform-rated 113 at two and 128 at three. On official ratings, he was a champion at two and also Europe's champion three-year-old miler.

His dam, You'resothrilling – whom Timeform rated 117 following her Group 2 Cherry Hinton Stakes victory at two – has made a dream start to her broodmare career with five significant runners from her first five foals – all of them by Galileo.

Gleneagles is her second born, and his older sister Marvellous won the Group 1 Irish 1000 Guineas. Number three is the Group 3 C L & M F Weld Park Stakes winner and Grade 1 Belmont Oaks Invitational Stakes third Coolmore, number four is the dual Group 2 Sandown Classic winner and Grade 1 Secretariat Stakes runner-up Taj Mahal, and her fifth foal is Happily. Timeform-rated 116 as a two-year-old when she won the Group 1 Moyglare Stud Stakes at the Curragh before avenging her brother's loss in France with a victory against the colts in the Group 1 Prix Jean-Luc Lagardere, she also won the Group 3 Silver Flash Stakes and was runner-up in the Group 2 Debutante Stakes. Happily was without a win in 2018 but was third to Billesdon Brook in the Group 1 1000 Guineas, third to Alpha Centauri in the Group 1 Irish 1000 Guineas, only beaten by a total of half a length when fourth to Laurens in the Group 1 Prix de Diane (French Oaks), and later failed by just a head to beat that latter classic star in the Group 1 Sun Chariot Stakes at Newmarket .

In addition to being a pattern-winning full-sister to the famously tough multiple Group 1 star and influential stallion Giant's Causeway, You'resothrilling is also a full-sister to Group 2-placed sprinter and leading New York-based sire Freud, and there is every reason to hope that Decorated Knight (by Galileo), the triple Group 1-winning son of her sister Pearling, will become a Group 1 sire from his Irish National Stud base. The offspring of Grade 1-placed multiple Grade 2 winner Mariah's Storm (by Rahy) also include Love Me Only (by Sadler's Wells), the dam of dual Derby-placed Group 2 Great Voltigeur Stakes scorer Storm The Stars (by Sea The Stars), whereas the third dam of Gleneagles is the Grade 3 winner Immense (by Roberto).

For a horse like Gleneagles it seems not a question of whether or not he will sire Group 1 winners but a matter of how many of them he will get. He is one of the most exciting stallion prospects to go to stud in Europe since Sea The Stars and Frankel.

SUMMARY DETAILS

Stood in 2016: Coolmore Stud, Ireland
Fee in 2016: €60,000
Career highlights: 7 wins inc 2000 Guineas (Gr1), Irish 2000 Guineas (Gr1), St James's Palace Stakes (Gr1), Goffs Vincent O'Brien National Stakes (Gr1), Futurity Stakes (Gr2), Tyros Stakes (Gr3), 3rd Prix Jean-Luc Lagardere Grand Criterium (Gr1)
Standing in 2019: Coolmore Stud, Ireland
Fee in 2019: €30,000
Stallions by his sire include: Cima De Triomphe (Gr1), Frankel (Gr1), Heliostatic (Gr1), Intello (Gr1), Nathaniel (Gr1), New

GLENEAGLES (IRE)

Approach (Gr1), Rip Van Winkle (Gr1), Roderic O'Connor (Gr1), Ruler Of The World (Gr1), Sixties Icon (Gr1), Soldier Of Fortune (Gr1), Teofilo (Gr1), Treasure Beach (Gr1)

GLENEAGLES (IRE) – bay 2012

Galileo (IRE)	Sadler's Wells (USA)	Northern Dancer (CAN)
		Fairy Bridge (USA)
	Urban Sea (USA)	Miswaki (USA)
		Allegretta
You'resothrilling (USA)	Storm Cat (USA)	Storm Bird (CAN)
		Terlingua (USA)
	Mariah's Storm (USA)	Rahy (USA)
		Immense (USA)

SALES YEARLINGS OF 2018

Sold in Euros

	bf - Nuit Polaire (by Kheleyf) - Arqana - August - €400,000
	bc - Unbelievable (by Fastnet Rock) - Goffs - October - €260,000
Bright Eyed Eagle (IRE)	chc - Euphrasia (by Windsor Knot) - Goffs - October - €220,000
	bc - Gotlandia (by Anabaa) - Arqana - August - €180,000
Angel of The Glen (FR)	bf - Archangel Gabriel (by Arch) - Arqana - August - €170,000
Glen Force (IRE)	bc - Lethal Quality (by Elusive Quality) - Goffs - October - €160,000
	bf - Mikkwa (by Elusive Quality) - Arqana - August - €150,000
Nordic (GER)	chc - Norwegian Pride (by Diktat) - Baden-Baden - August - €150,000
	chf - Pipalong (by Pips Pride) - Goffs - October - €150,000
	bc - Alive Alive Oh (by Duke Of Marmalade) - Goffs - October - €140,000
	chc - Brasileira (by Dubai Destination) - Arqana - August - €115,000
	bc - Elle Woods (by Lawman) - Goffs - October - €110,000

	bf - Obama Rule (by Danehill Dancer) - Goffs - October - €110,000
	grc - Convocate (by Exchange Rate) - Goffs - October - €90,000
Dream Round (IRE)	chf - Mythie (by Octagonal) - Goffs - October - €82,000
	bf - Kiss Of Spring (by Dansili) - Arqana - August - €80,000 (p/s)
	bc - One Chance (by Invincible Spirit) - Tatts IRE - September - €70,000
	chf - Daltiana (by Selkirk) - Osarus - September - €62,000
	bf - Elitiste (by Danehill Dancer) - Arqana - August - €50,000
	chc - Fluvial (by Exceed And Excel) - Goffs - October - €50,000
	bf - Vadirima (by Selkirk) - Arqana - October - €38,000
	chc - Bora Blues (by Peintre Celebre) - Tatts IRE - September - €30,000
	bf - Cap Coz (by Indian Ridge) - Goffs - October - €20,000
	bf - Crossover (by Cape Cross) - Goffs - October - €18,000 (p/s)
	bc - Lookup (by Inchinor) - Arqana - October - €12,000

Sold in Guineas

	bf - Tarbela (by Grand Lodge) - Tattersalls - October - 500,000gns
Sparkling Olly (IRE)	bf - Sogno Verdc (by Green Desert) - Tattersalls - October - 300,000gns
	bc - Bridal Dance (by Danehill Dancer) - Tattersalls - November - 240,000gns
	bf - Fusion (by Cape Cross) - Tattersalls - October - 200,000gns
Mente Hermosa (GB)	bf - Que Puntual (by Contested Bid) - Tattersalls - October - 200,000gns
Mafia Power (GB)	bc - Rivara (by Red Ransom) - Tattersalls - October - 200,000gns

Wild Place (IRE)   bc - No Explaining (by Azamour) -
Tattersalls - October - 190,000gns
bf - Sitara (by Salse) - Tattersalls -
October - 115,000gns
bf - Dingle View (by Mujadil) -
Tattersalls - October - 90,000gns
bf - Liberally (by Statue Of Liberty) -
Tattersalls - October - 75,000gns (p/s)
bc - Sweet Coincidence (by Mujahid) -
Tattersalls - October - 72,000gns
chc - Precious Dream (by Mr Greeley) -
Tattersalls - October - 62,000gns
chc - Cape Columbine (by Diktat) -
Tattersalls - October - 60,000gns
bc - Bratislava (by Dr Fong) - Tattersalls
- October - 57,000gns
chc - Hallouella (by Halling) - Tattersalls
- October - 55,000gns
bf - Rive Gauche (by Fastnet Rock) -
Tattersalls - October - 55,000gns
bc - Coquet (by Sir Percy) - Tattersalls -
October - 42,000gns
chf - Crystal Valkyrie (by Danehill) -
Tattersalls - November - 37,000gns
bc - Don't Forget Faith (by Victory
Gallop) - Tattersalls - February -
28,000gns

Silence Please (IRE)   b/brf - Crazy Volume (by
Machiavellian) - Tattersalls - October -
27,000gns
bf - Dubai Media (by Songandaprayer) -
Tattersalls - October - 25,000gns
bc - Don't Forget Faith (by Victory
Gallop) - Tattersalls - October -
16,000gns
bc - Araqella (by Oasis Dream) -
Tattersalls - October - 10,000gns (p/s)
bc - Talawat (by Cape Cross) -
Tattersalls - November - 5,000gns

Sold in Pounds

Mahanakhon Power (GB)   bc - Lady Eclair (by Danehill Dancer) - Goffs UK - August - £380,000

Bound For Heaven (GB) bf - Sugar Mill (by Oasis Dream) - Goffs UK - August - £140,000

bc - Snowfields (by Raven's Pass) - Goffs UK - August - £100,000

bc - Native Picture (by Kodiac) - Goffs UK - August - £42,000

Not Sold (inc. vendor buy-backs)

bc - Acquainted (by Shamardal) - Tattersalls - October

bc - Aristocratic Lady (by Kris S) - Tattersalls - November

bf - Better Not Cry (by Street Cry) - Keeneland - September

bc - Caphene (by Sakhee) - Tattersalls - October

bf - Deter (by Nayef) - Goffs - October

bf - Fondly (by Dansili) - Tattersalls - November

bc - Four Eleven (by Arch) - Arqana - August

brf - Lips Arrow (by Big Shuffle) - Baden-Baden - August

bc - Love Excelling (by Polish Precedent) - Tattersalls - October

bc - Milady (by Shamardal) - Tattersalls - October

b/brf - Miss Lacey (by Diktat) - Tattersalls - October

b/brf - Miss Lahar (by Clodovil) - Tattersalls - October

brf - Red Lips (by Areion) - Baden-Baden - August

bf - Street Style (by Rock Of Gibraltar) - Tattersalls - October

Tabera (GB)   bf - Temida (by Oratorio) - Tattersalls - October

GLENEAGLES (IRE)

GOLDEN HORN (GB)

Green Desert forged one of two powerful branches of the Danzig (by Northern Dancer) sire line, and there are early signs that three divisions of the late Nunnery Stud's one may be emerging. Right now it is the Invincible Spirit offshoot that is strongest, while the Oasis Dream one is yielding blacktype sires with, as yet, just one standout among them. All of this may change.

The third one is more of a bud, but we may be talking about a Cape Cross branch in the next decade. Timeform 140-rated Sea The Stars, his most brilliant son, is one of Europe's leading sires and has young stallion sons of his own. Awtaad (yearlings) and Golden Horn are in early stages of their stud careers, Guignol is a new French-based sire in 2019, and the other pattern winners backing up those Group 1 aces include Group 2 scorer Moohaajim whose low double-digit number of first-crop runners in 2018 yielded seven winners, headed by four-time scorer Hard Taskmaster and the unbeaten dual winner Irene May.

Narrow conqueror of Storm The Stars in an eight-and-a-half-furlong Nottingham maiden on his only start at two, Golden Horn went on to become a European champion at three, earning a Timeform rating of 134 and their Horse of the Year accolade. He kicked off that campaign with victory in the Listed Feilden Stakes over nine furlongs at Newmarket, followed-up with an impressive defeat of Jack Hobbs in the Group 2 Dante Stakes over the extended 10 furlongs at York, and then became the subject of usual debate at that time of the year: would this exciting colt stay the Derby distance?

In my May 2015 analysis in *The Irish Field*, titled "Golden Horn bred to stay Derby distance", I noted the speed elements of his pedigree that were leading many to think he would not last the distance, but also pointed out the strong middle-distance aspects of his pedigree, its "record when it comes to producing horses who can be effective at around a mile and a half."

His unraced dam, Fleche D'Or (by Dubai Destination), is a half-sister to the Group 1 Coronation Stakes winner and Group 1 Queen Elizabeth II Stakes runner-up Rebecca Sharp (by Machiavellian), but the middle-distance stakes winners Mystic Knight (by Caerleon) and Hidden Hope (by Daylami) are close-up too, and a three-parts-sister to the dam of Golden Horn was a multiple winner at around 12 furlongs. I closed the piece by saying: "There are, of course, no guarantees when it comes to pedigrees, and it is entirely possible that Golden Horn could come cruising two out at Epsom only to falter when his stamina is put to the test. But, his pedigree lengthens the odds of that scenario unfolding, and if he really is the horse he looked to be that day at York, then Golden Horn could be one of the brightest stars of 2015."

He beat Jack Hobbs by farther at Epsom than he had done at York, and while that rival went to Ireland to take the Irish Derby, his dual conqueror dropped back to 10 furlongs to beat The Grey Gatsby in style in the Group 1 Coral-Eclipse at Sandown. His neck defeat by Arabian Queen at York was a shock and a long way below his form, but he bounced back to beat Found in the Group 1 Irish Champion Stakes before taking the Group 1 Prix de l'Arc de Triomphe by two lengths from Flintshire, and then lost out by half a length to his Leopardstown victim in the Grade 1 Breeders' Cup Turf at Keeneland.

There are no stallions evident in the first three generations of his family – the best winners have all been fillies or geldings – but he is a top-class son of a leading Green Desert stallion, he is by the sire of outstanding racehorse and stallion Sea The Stars, and there is an eye-catching mix of speed and stamina in his pedigree. Golden Horn's better two-year-olds are likely to be seen out in the second half of the season, with some of them being blacktype horses, but his strongest record promises to be with three-year-olds and older horses. Depending on whether it is the speed or stamina elements of both their sire's and dam's pedigree that his offspring get, it can be expected that some will be milers, while others will prove most effective at middle-distances, and some may stay farther – covering the full classic range. He stands at Dalham Hall Stud, there were 84 foals in his first crop, and a double-digit number of his initial offspring fetched a six-figure sum in the auction ring in 2018, headed by a 550,000gns colt.

SUMMARY DETAILS

Stood in 2016: Dalham Hall Stud, England
Fee in 2016: £60,000
Career highlights: 7 wins inc Prix de l'Arc de Triomphe (Gr1), Derby (Gr1), Coral-Eclipse Stakes (Gr1), Qipco Irish Champion

Stakes (Gr1), Dante Stakes (Gr2) Fielden Stakes (L), 2nd
Juddmonte International Stakes (Gr1), Breeders' Cup Turf (Gr1)
Standing in 2019: Dalham Hall Stud, England
Fee in 2019: £50,000
Other stallions by his sire include: Sea The Stars (Gr1),
Behkabad (winners), Confuchias (winners), Halicarnassus
(winners), Moohaajim (winners), Recharge (winners), Jet Away
(3yo in 2019), Golden Horn (2yo), Awtaad (yearlings), Karpino
(foals), Guignol (new)

GOLDEN HORN (GB) – bay 2012

Cape Cross (IRE)	Green Desert (USA)	Danzig (USA)
		Foreign Courier (USA)
	Park Appeal	Ahonoora
		Balidaress
Fleche D'Or (GB)	Dubai Destination (USA)	Kingmambo (USA)
		Mysterial (USA)
	Nuryana	Nureyev (USA)
		Loralane

SALES YEARLINGS OF 2018
Sold in Euros

	brc - Ninfea (by Selkirk) - Baden-Baden - August - €205,000
	bc - Alta Lilea (by Galileo) - Arqana - August - €200,000
	bf - First Fleet (by Woodman) - Arqana - August - €200,000
	bf - Quezon Sun (by Monsun) - Arqana - August - €200,000
St Clerans (IRE)	bf - Discreet Brief (by Darshaan) - Goffs - October - €170,000
	bf - Longing To Dance (by Danehill Dancer) - Arqana - August - €170,000
Hysterique (GB)	bf - Rose Et Noire (by Dansili) - Arqana - October - €120,000
	bf - Simonetta (by Lil's Boy) - Tatts IRE - September - €78,000
	grf - Sayfoonisa (by Azamour) - Arqana - August - €32,000

brc - Candle Lit (by Duke Of
Marmalade) - Goffs - October - €17,000

Sold in Guineas

	bc - Astonishing (by Galileo) - Tattersalls - October - 550,000gns
Trebizond (GB)	bc - Night Frolic (by Night Shift) - Tattersalls - October - 300,000gns
Golden Pine (IRE)	bc - Snow Pine (by Dalakhani) - Tattersalls - October - 280,000gns
Mark Of Gold (GB)	bc - Polly's Mark (by Mark Of Esteem) - Tattersalls - October - 220,000gns
Thumur (USA)	bc - Time Being (by Zamindar) - Tattersalls - October - 220,000gns
Solar Screen (IRE)	grc - Screen Star (by Tobougg) - Tattersalls - October - 210,000gns
Court of Appeal (IRE)	bc - Gwael (by A.P. Indy) - Tattersalls - October - 200,000gns
El Pelegrino (GB)	bc - La Dorotea (by Lope De Vega) - Tattersalls - October - 200,000gns
	bc - Polarized (by Medicean) - Tattersalls - October - 200,000gns
Lady G (IRE)	bf - Hikari (by Galileo) - Tattersalls - October - 150,000gns (p/s)
	bf - Lovely Pass (by Raven's Pass) - Tattersalls - October - 150,000gns
	bf - Nina Celebre (by Peintre Celebre) - Tattersalls - October - 130,000gns
Brackish (GB)	bc - Delizia (by Dark Angel) - Tattersalls - October - 110,000gns
Influx (IRE)	bc - Steel Princess (by Danehill) - Tattersalls - October - 100,000gns
	bf - Free Rein (by Dansili) - Tattersalls - October - 95,000gns
Golden Lips (IRE)	bf - Lady Penko (by Archipenko) - Tattersalls - October - 80,000gns (p/s)
	bf - Gaze (by Galileo) - Tattersalls - October - 75,000gns (p/s)
	brc - Liber Nauticus (by Azamour) - Tattersalls - October - 75,000gns

Dutch Schultz (GB)   bc - Karpina (by Pivotal) - Tattersalls - October - 65,000gns
bc - Kitty Wells (by Sadler's Wells) - Tattersalls - November - 55,000gns
bc - Dorcas Lane (by Norse Dancer) - Tattersalls - October - 52,000gns
bc - Alfajer (by Mount Nelson) - Tattersalls - November - 40,000gns
bc - What A Picture (by Peintre Celebre) - Tattersalls - November - 40,000gns
bf - Festoso (by Diesis) - Tattersalls - October - 35,000gns
bf - Morzine (by Miswaki) - Tattersalls - November - 12,000gns

Not Sold (inc. vendor buy-backs)

bc - Bella Lulu (by Iffraaj) - Tattersalls - October
Presidential Sweet (ITY)   bf - Biz Bar (by Tobougg) - Tattersalls - October
bf - Iowa Falls (by Dansili) - Arqana - August
Moonlight And Gold (GB)   bf - Molly Malone (by Lomitas) - Arqana - August
bc - Sefroua (by Kingmambo) - Arqana - August

96

GUTAIFAN (IRE)

It is disappointing when a talented two-year-old doesn't return to the track at three, going straight to stud instead. Fasliyev was injured, so that was understandable, and Holy Roman Emperor was reportedly being prepared for the classics when shipped to stud to replace the infertile George Washington. Teofilo remained in training at three but was unable to return to the track due to a setback, but he covered his first book at four. Two of that trio became leading sires, and classic sires, whereas the other one was one of those stallions who make a flashy start with first-crop juveniles only to have that spark peter out. He has, however, sired many winners and some talented stakes winners.

Dark Angel (by Acclamation), on the other hand, was a somewhat lowly-rated Group 1 Middle Park Stakes winner who was surprisingly packed off to stud rather than enter training at three. This was before the enhanced three-year-old sprint programme that has been such a tremendous addition to the calendar. The move proved to be a huge success, and he now commands one of the highest fees in Europe. He is the sire of the Group/Grade 1 stars Battaash, Harry Angel, Hunt, Lethal Force, Mecca's Angel, Persuasive, and Raging Bull, he has a growing string of sons at stud, and it could just be a matter of time before he gets his first Group 1 classic star.

Those sire sons include Lethal Force, Tough As Nails, 2018's freshmen Alhebayeb and Heeraat, and also Gutaifan, a leading sprint juvenile who, like his sire, covered his first book of mares as a three-year-old. The latter stands alongside his sire at Yeomanstown Stud. Gutaifan's Timeform rating of 117 is higher than that of his sire (113), he was a Group 1-placed dual Group 2 scorer, finished down the field in the Group 1 Prix de l'Abbaye de Longchamp on his only time out of the frame, and from just over 200 mares mares in his initial season has just over 150 individuals in his first crop.

He is the best of eight winners out of Alikhlas (by Lahib), his dam's siblings include the listed scorer and dual 12-furlong Group 2-placed filly Sahool (by Unfuwain), and also the dams of Maraahel (by Alzao) and Ventura Storm (by Zoffany). The former, a dual Group 2 Hardwicke Stakes winner, was placed in a string of the top 10-12 furlong Group 1 events, while the latter, a

12-furlong Group 1 scorer in Italy and now Group 1-placed in Australia, was runner-up in the Group 1 St Leger.

So Gutaifan represents what has been a stamina-oriented immediate family, and it seems that his sire's speed must have combined with that from the third generation of his pedigree, even though his unraced third dam, Manal (by Luthier), was a full-sister to the Group 1-placed middle-distance pattern winners Tip Moss and Twig Moss. There you will find Group 3 Princess Margaret Stakes winner Muhbubh (by Blushing Groom), seven-furlong Group/Grade 2 scorers Kayrawan (by Mr Prospector) and Sayedah (by Darshaan), and six-furlong Group 2 winners Magical Memory (by Zebedee), Haatef (by Danzig), and Asfurah (by Dayjur), among others of note.

All of this is going to make Gutaifan an interesting prospect as a stallion, and, like his sire, he will probably get his best winners at anywhere from five to 10 furlongs. His initial yearlings found buyers at all levels of the market, with several of them making six-figure sums. Many will likely reach the racetrack in 2019, some will no doubt be early types, and the weight of numbers should help him to figure prominently in the freshman sires tables, by winners, races won, and by earnings. He could also be one to watch in those lucrative sales races. It is striking that the Dark Angel stallions with runners have yet to show the potential to become sires of note, but this may change as some of his more strongly bred sons get to that stage of their stud careers, or if those early ones begin to make progress in 2019. The many supporters of Gutaifan will be hoping that he becomes one who will make the breakthrough.

SUMMARY DETAILS

Stood in 2016: Yeomanstown Stud, Ireland
Fee in 2016: €12,500
Career highlights: 4 wins inc Flying Childers Stakes (Gr2), Prix Robert Papin (Gr2), 2nd Prix Morny (Gr1)
Standing in 2019: Yeomanstown Stud, Ireland
Fee in 2019: €10,000
Stallions by his sire include: Alhebayeb (winners), Heeraat (winners), Lethal Force (winners), Tough As Nails (winners), Gutaifan (2yo), Estidhkaar (yearlings), Markaz (ycarlings), Birchwood (foals), Harry Angel (new)

GUTAIFAN (IRE) – grey 2013

Dark Angel (IRE)	Acclamation (GB)	Royal Applause (GB)
		Princess Athena
	Midnight Angel (GB)	Machiavellian (USA)
		Night At Sea
Alikhlas (GB)	Lahib (USA)	Riverman (USA)
		Lady Cutlass (USA)
	Mathaayl (USA)	Shadeed (USA)
		Manal (FR)

SALES YEARLINGS OF 2018

Sold in Euros

Love Powerful (IRE) bf - Montefino (by Shamardal) - Goffs - October - €360,000

bc - Alyaafel (by Cape Cross) - Arqana - August - €170,000

Written Broadcast (IRE) grc - Teeline (by Exceed And Excel) - Goffs - October - €150,000

bc - Bali Breeze (by Common Grounds) - Goffs - October - €105,000

brc - Oh Sedulous (by Lawman) - Goffs - October - €95,000

With Respect (IRE) grc - More Respect (by Spectrum) - Goffs - October - €85,000

bf - Lillebonne (by Danehill Dancer) - Arqana - August - €65,000

bc - Divine Design (by Barathea) - Goffs - October - €55,000 (p/s)

blc - Gerash (by Layman) - Goffs - October - €52,000

bc - Anadolu (by Statue Of Liberty) - Goffs - October - €50,000 (p/s)

br/grc - Hairicin (by Hurricane Run) - Goffs - October - €40,000

grc - Teeline (by Exceed And Excel) - Goffs - February - €40,000

grc - Boucheron (by Galileo) - Goffs - February - €38,000

bc - Spicy (by Footstepsinthesand) - Tatts IRE - September - €38,000

bc - Whatever You Do (by Barathea) -
Tatts IRE - September - €32,000
bc - Anadolu (by Statue Of Liberty) -
Goffs - February - €31,000
bc - Lost Shilling (by Noverre) - Goffs -
February - €31,000
bf - Mansiya (by Vettori) - Goffs -
October - €27,000
bc - She's A Character (by Invincible
Spirit) - Tatts IRE - September -
€27,000
grf - Coco Rouge (by Shamardal) -
Goffs - October - €26,000
grf - Best New Show (by Clodovil) -
Goffs - October - €25,000
bc - Suite (by Invincible Spirit) - Goffs -
October - €25,000
grc - Cockney Rhyme (by Cockney
Rebel) - Goffs - February - €23,000
brc - City Dazzler (by Elusive City) -
Tatts IRE - September - €20,000

Ocasio Cortez (IRE) grf - Novel Fun (by Noverre) - Tatts
IRE - September - €20,000
grc - Peace Talks (by Pivotal) - Tatts
IRE - September - €20,000
brf - Yet Again (by Oasis Dream) -
Tatts IRE - September - €20,000

Garigliano (FR) bc - Green Ridge (by Green Tune) -
Arqana - October - €18,000
bc - Sabinillas (by Clodovil) - Tatts IRE
- September - €18,000
bc - Lathaat (by Dubai Destination) -
Goffs - February - €17,000
grc - Can Dance (by Manduro) - Arqana
- August - €16,000
grf - Holly's Kid (by Pulpit) - Tatts IRE
- September - €16,000
bf - Classic Style (by Desert Style) -
Tatts IRE - September - €15,000

brf - Naruko (by Street Cry) - Tatts IRE - September - €15,000

brc - Miss America (by Bernardini) - Tatts IRE - September - €13,500

bc - Treasure The Lady (by Indian Ridge) - Goffs - February - €13,500

grf - Asgardella (by Duke Of Marmalade) - Goffs - October - €13,000

grc - Burning Dawn (by Bernstein) - Tatts IRE - September - €12,000 (p/s)

Odyssey Girl (IRE)   brf - Lady Marita (by Dandy Man) - Tatts IRE - September - €12,000

grc - Miss Mary (by Multiplex) - Goffs - November - €10,000

bc - Heeby Heeby (by Lawman) - Tatts IRE - September - €9,500

bf - Valentina Guest (by Be My Guest) - Goffs - February - €9,000

bf - Brosnan (by Champs Elysees) - Goffs - October - €8,000

bc - Galileos Daughter (by Galileo) - Tatts IRE - September - €8,000

bf - Nectar Grey (by Mastercraftsman) - SGA - September - €8,000

grf - Tranquil Sky (by Intikhab) - Goffs - October - €8,000

Real Fan (FR)   bf - Reality (by Slickly) - Baden-Baden - August - €7,000

bc - Great Artist (by Desert Prince) - Arqana - October - €6,000

bf - La Reine Mambo (by High Yield) - Goffs - October - €6,000

grc - Ophelia's Song (by Halling) - Tatts IRE - September - €5,000 (p/s)

bf - Wonderful Town (by Bernstein) - Goffs - October - €5,000

grf - Vale Of Belvoir (by Mull Of Kintyre) - Goffs - November - €4,500

bc - With A Twist (by Excellent Art) - Goffs - October - €4,500

GUTAIFAN (IRE)

grc - Scarborough Lily (by Dansili) -
Goffs - November - €3,500
bf - Timbre (by Dubai Destination) -
Tatts IRE - September - €2,000
grf - Stained Glass (by Dansili) - Goffs -
November - €1,000
b/brc - Ursula (by Namid) - Goffs -
November - €1,000

Sold in Guineas

grc - Arabian Pearl (by Refuse To Bend)
- Tattersalls - October - 225,000gns
bc - Cape Factor (by Oratorio) -
Tattersalls - October - 200,000gns
Lady Goldfrapp (IRE)   bf - Supreme Seductress (by Montjeu) -
Tattersalls - October - 200,000gns
bf - Anna Law (by Lawman) -
Tattersalls - October - 180,000gns
bc - Dust Flicker (by Suave Dancer) -
Tattersalls - October - 140,000gns
Glorious Rio (IRE)   bc - Renaissance Rio (by Captain Rio) -
Tattersalls - October - 80,000gns
bc - Mimisel (by Selkirk) - Tattersalls -
October - 75,000gns
grc - Ms Sasha Malia (by Verglas) -
Tattersalls - October - 75,000gns
bc - C'Est Ma Souer (by Oratorio) -
Tattersalls - November - 55,000gns
A Day At The Races (IRE) bf - Al Andalyya (by Kingmambo) -
Tattersalls - October - 50,000gns
grc - Carallia (by Common Grounds) -
Tattersalls - October - 50,000gns
brc - Boucheron (by Galileo) -
Tattersalls - October - 48,000gns
bc - Island Sunset (by Trans Island) -
Tattersalls - October - 45,000gns
Vintage Polly (IRE)   brf - Payphone (by Anabaa) - Tattersalls
- October - 45,000gns
Kidda (GB)   grc - Lily Again (by American Post) -
Tattersalls - October - 43,000gns

103

Angel Grey (IRE)   grf - Violet's Gift (by Cadeaux Genereux) - Tattersalls - October - 38,000gns
grf - Ellasha (by Shamardal) - Tattersalls - October - 30,000gns
bc - Scent Of Summer (by Rock Hard Ten) - Tattersalls - October - 28,000gns
grc - Pilosa (by Arcano) - Tattersalls - October - 24,000gns
grc - Cockney Rhyme (by Cockney Rebel) - Tattersalls - October - 21,000gns
bc - Galileo's Star (by Galileo) - Tattersalls - October - 21,000gns

Silver Grace (IRE)   grf - Maybe Grace (by Hawk Wing) - Tattersalls - October - 20,000gns
grc - Scarlet Rosefinch (by Cockney Rebel) - Tattersalls - October - 20,000gns
bc - Streamer (by Medicean) - Tattersalls - October - 18,000gns

Coconut Sugar (IRE)   bf - Murrieta (by Docksider) - Tattersalls - October - 12,000gns
grf - Sveva (by Danehill Dancer) - Tattersalls - October - 9,000gns
grf - Lovely Thought (by Dubai Destination) - Tattersalls - October - 8,000gns

Woodcock (IRE)   grg - Tooley Woods (by Cape Cross) - Tattersalls - October - 8,000gns
grf - Doula (by Gone West) - Tattersalls - October - 4,500gns
grc - Champs d'Or (by Champs Elysees) - Tattersalls - October - 3,000gns
grc - Cosenza (by Bahri) - Tattersalls - October - 2,000gns

Sold in Pounds
Khalaf (GB)   bc - Dominatrix (by Whipper) - Goffs UK - August - £100,000

GUTAIFAN (IRE)

Atomflot (IRE)	bc - Xema (by Danehill) - Goffs UK - August - £100,000
	grc - Beguiler (by Refuse To Bend) - Goffs UK - August - £75,000
Cold Comfort (IRE)	bf - Tamarisk (by Selkirk) - Goffs UK - August - £70,000
Krabi (GB)	bf - Miskin Diamond (by Diamond Green) - Goffs UK - August - £62,000
Convincer (IRE)	bc - Deora De (by Night Shift) - Goffs UK - August - £58,000
	bc - Crystal Morning (by Cape Cross) - Goffs UK - August - £50,000
Funny Little Ways (IRE)	grf - Midnight Oasis (by Oasis Dream) - Goffs UK - August - £48,000
	grf - Rahaala (by Indian Ridge) - Goffs UK - August - £45,000
	bc - Rumline (by Royal Applause) - Goffs UK - August - £42,000
	brc - Aja (by Excellent Art) - Goffs UK - August - £40,000
Zellerate (IRE)	bc - Ride For Roses (by Barathea) - Goffs UK - August - £33,000
	bc - Lathaat (by Dubai Destination) - Goffs UK - August - £32,000
	bf - Worthington (by Kodiac) - Goffs UK - August - £30,000
	grc - Margarita (by Marju) - Goffs UK - August - £28,000
	bc - Spirited Acclaim (by Acclamation) - Goffs UK - August - £26,000
	bc - Coursing (by Kyllachy) - Goffs UK - August - £20,000
	grf - Rugged Up (by Marju) - Goffs UK - August - £20,000
	brc - Rayon Rouge (by Manduro) - Goffs UK - August - £18,000 (p/s)
	bf - Avenbury (by Mount Nelson) - Goffs UK - August - £15,000 (p/s)
	bc - St Athan (by Authorized) - Tatts IRE Ascot - September - £15,000

Hoy Lake (GB)	bc - Flames To Dust (by Oasis Dream) - Goffs UK - August - £13,500
	grc - Silken Satinwood (by Refuse To Bend) - Goffs UK - August - £12,000
Rat N Mouse (IRE)	grf - Rhythm And Rhyme (by Elnadim) - Goffs UK - August - £8,000
	bc - Green Poppy (by Green Desert) - Goffs UK - August - £7,000
	blc - Edge Of Love (by Kyllachy) - Goffs UK - August - £5,000
	grf - Kyanight (by Kodiac) - Goffs UK - August - £5,500

Not Sold (inc. vendor buy-backs)

	bf - Always Gentle (by Redback) - Tattersalls - October
	brc - Aqraan (by In The Wings) - Tatts IRE - September
	grf - Bella Ophelia (by Baltic King) - Goffs UK - August
	bc - Boom And Boom (by Lawman) - Tattersalls - October
	bc - Caribbean Queen (by Celtic Swing) - Goffs - November
	brc - City Dazzler (by Elusive City) - Goffs - February
	bc - Dame Alicia (by Sadler's Wells) - Goffs - October
	grf - Dinka Raja (by Woodman) - Tatts IRE - September
Sweet Design (IRE)	brf - Dixiedoodledandy (by Desert Style) - Goffs - February
	bf - Exclusion (by Include) - Tatts IRE - September
	grf - Holly's Kid (by Pulpit) - Goffs - February
	bc - Lady Catherine (by Bering) - Goffs - November
	grf - Love Action (by Motivator) - Tattersalls - October

	bf - Mags Rock (by Fastnet Rock) - Goffs - February
Prissy Missy (IRE)	bf - Maracuja (by Medicean) - Tatts IRE - September
	bc - Musica E Magia (by King's Theatre) - Goffs - November
	bc - Musically (by Singspiel) - Tatts IRE - September
	grc - Princess Of Troy (by Tiger Hill) - Goffs UK - August
	bf - Queenofthenorth (by Halling) - Tattersalls - October
	bc - Rich Gift (by Cadeaux Genereux) - Tatts IRE - September
	bf - Salmon Rose (by Iffraaj) - Tatts IRE - September
	grc - Soxy Doxy (by Hawk Wing) - Goffs UK - August
	brf - The Oldladysays No (by Perugino) - Goffs - November
Ivy Garden (IRE)	bc - Treasure The Lady (by Indian Ridge) - Tatts IRE - September
	bc - Twiggy's Girl (by Manduro) - Tatts IRE - September
	bc - Whatever You Do (by Barathea) - Goffs - February

FRESHMAN SIRES OF 2019

HALLOWED CROWN (AUS)

A Group 1 winner over seven and eight furlongs in Australia, Hallowed Crown stood at Kildangan Stud for two seasons – he had 64 foals in the northern hemisphere half his first crop – but did not return from native land in 2018. He is a son of the Grade 1 Kentucky Derby hero Street Sense (by Street Cry) and represents the Machiavellian branch of the broader Mr Prospector (by Raise a Native) line. He also has the attraction of being a half-brother to a newly crowned Group 1 sire.

That sibling is the Australian Group 3 scorer Needs Further (by Encosta De Lago) whose second-crop daughter Mystic Journey made it four blacktype wins in a row when easily beating the males in the Group 1 Australian Guineas over a mile at Flemington at the start of March. A fortnight later, the Adam Trinder-trained filly confirmed her position as a rising star when taking on her elders in the inaugural A$5 million All-Star Mile, landing the prize by a length and a quarter from Hartnell and with another multiple Group 1 ace, Alizee, a short-head back in third.

The brothers are out of the Group 3 winner and Group 1 Golden Slipper Stakes runner-up Crowned Glory (by Danehill), and their grandam Significant Moment (by Bletchingly) is a half-sister to the mighty Zabeel (by Sir Tristram). That New Zealand-bred Group 1 winner and Cambridge Stud stallion has been a prolific champion sire, and that augurs well for the prospects of his young relation.

He, Significant Moment, and Group 1 scorer Baryshnikov (by Kenmare) are out of the unraced Nureyev (by Northern Dancer) mare Lady Giselle, and she, in turn, was out of French listed winner Valderna (by Val De Loir). That mare's siblings feature classic-placed Group 1 Cheveley Park Stakes winner Durtal (by Lyphard) – the dam of dual Group 1 Gold Cup hero Gildoran (by Rheingold) – and Detroit (by Riverman) who was the first Group 1 Prix de l'Arc de Triomphe star to become the dam of an Arc winner. Her star son was Group 1 sire Carnegie (by Sadler's Wells), and Detroit's feat was eventually duplicated by Urban Sea and her son Sea The Stars.

It will be interesting to see how Hallowed Crown's stock are received and how they perform in Europe, but with his relationship to Zabeel, there is every reason to think that he will become a sire of Group 1 winners in the southern hemisphere, regardless of how his European offspring turn out.

SUMMARY DETAILS

Stood in 2016: Kildangan Stud, Ireland
Fee in 2016: €7,000
Career highlights: 6 wins inc Golden Rose Stakes (Gr1), Randwick Guineas (Gr1), Hobartville Stakes (Gr2), Run to the Rose (Gr3), Kindergarten Stakes (Gr3), 3rd Rosehill Guineas (Gr1)
Standing in 2019: in Australia
Stallions by his sire include: Street Life (winners), Cigar Street (2yo), Hallowed Crown (2yo), Elnaawi (yearlings), Street Strategy (yearlings), Thunder Down Under (foals), The Lieutenant (new)

HALLOWED CROWN (AUS) – bay 2011

Street Sense (USA)	Street Cry (IRE)	Machiavellian (USA)
		Helen Street
	Bedazzle (USA)	Dixieland Band (USA)
		Majestic Legend (USA)
Crowned Glory (AUS)	Danehill (USA)	Danzig (USA)
		Razyana (USA)
	Significant Moment (AUS)	Bletchingly (AUS)
		Lady Giselle (FR)

SALES YEARLINGS OF 2018

Sold in Euros

Castleton Girl (IRE)	bf - Lauren's Girl (by Bushranger) - Tatts IRE - September - €62,000
The Perfect Crown (IRE)	bc - Perfect Fun (by Marju) - Goffs - February - €55,000
Scout's Honor (GER)	bf - Scouting (by New Approach) - Baden-Baden - August - €49,000
Ya Ya Baby (IRE)	bf - Standout (by Robellino) - Goffs - October - €38,000
	bc - Chica Whopa (by Oasis Dream) - Tatts IRE - September - €35,000
	bc - Alpine (by Rail Link) - Tatts IRE - September - €24,000
Va Tutto Bene (IRE)	bc - Cherry Creek (by Montjeu) - Goffs - October - €23,000

	brc - Gemma's Pearl (by Marju) - Goffs - October - €16,000
Hallowed Song (FR)	bf - Fammi Sognare (by Bertolini) - Arqana - October - €8,000
Weeds (IRE)	bf - Crystal Bull (by Holy Bull) - SGA - September - €7,000
	bc - Semiquaver (by Mark Of Esteem) - Goffs - October - €7,000
	bf - Hermia (by Cape Cross) - Goffs - November - €6,000
	bf - Blue Dune (by Invincible Spirit) - Tatts IRE - September - €5,500
	bc - Tranquil Spirit (by Invincible Spirit) - Tatts IRE - September - €5,000
	bf - Blue Dune (by Invincible Spirit) - Goffs - February - €4,500
	bc - Ava's World (by Desert Prince) - Goffs - November - €4,000
	bf - Oasis Fire (by Oasis Dream) - Tatts IRE - September - €4,000
	bf - Timeless Whisper (by Footstepsinthesand) - Goffs - November - €3,500
	bc - Virgin Hawk (by Silver Hawk) - Goffs - February - €3,500
	bf - Freezing Love (by Danzig) - Goffs - November - €1,500
	grf - Dalaway (by Dalakhani) - Goffs - November - €1,000
	bc - Ivy Batty (by King's Best) - Goffs - November - €1,000
	bf - Supreme Spirit (by Invincible Spirit) - Goffs - November - €1,000 (p/s)

Sold in Guineas

| Karibana (IRE) | bc - Queen Wasp (by Shamardal) - Tattersalls - October - 52,000gns |
| The Perfect Crown (IRE) | bc - Perfect Fun (by Marju) - Tattersalls - October - 40,000gns |

bf - Snowdrops (by Gulch) - Tattersalls
- October - 30,000gns
bc - Elbow Beach (by Choisir) -
Tattersalls - October - 11,000gns
bf - Zumurudah (by Dubawi) -
Tattersalls - October - 6,500gns
bc - Peaceful Soul (by Dynaformer) -
Tattersalls - October - 4,500gns
bc - Happy Wedding (by Green Tune) -
Tattersalls - November - 3,000gns
bf - All Rounder (by Mizzen Mast) -
Tattersalls - October - 1,000gns (p/s)
bf - Hikayati (by Iffraaj) - Tattersalls -
October - 800gns
bf - Joyful Friend (by Dubawi) -
Tattersalls - October - 800gns

Sold in Pounds

bc - Hflah (by Dubawi) - Goffs UK -
August - £26,000
bc - Phi Phi (by Fasliyev) - Goffs UK -
August - £26,000
bf - Indian Angel (by Indian Ridge) -
Goffs UK - August - £14,000
bc - My Girl Lisa (by With Approval) -
Goffs UK - August - £14,000
bc - Tagula Mon (by Tagula) - Goffs
UK - August - £6,500
bc - Yaqootah (by Gone West) - Tatts
IRE Ascot - September - £3,000

Not Sold (inc. vendor buy-backs)

bf - Allofus (by Celtic Swing) - Goffs -
November
bf - Beach Candy (by Footstepsinthesand) - Tatts IRE - September
b/brc - Blue Moonstone (by English
Channel) - Goffs - November
bf - Deryshicca (by Danehill Dancer) -
Goffs - November

bf - Fastnet Lady (by Fastnet Rock) - Goffs - November

bf - Gold Approach (by New Approach) - Tattersalls - November

bf - Kinnego (by Sri Pekan) - Goffs - November

bc - Magical Rose (by Elusive City) - Goffs - February

bc - Makheelah (by Dansili) - Tatts IRE - September

bc - Mataji (by Desert Prince) - Goffs UK - August

bf - Meanwhile (by Haafhd) - Tattersalls - November

bc - Methayel (by Araafa) - Tatts IRE Ascot - September

bf - Sarah Ann (by Orpen) - Goffs - November

grf - She's A Minx (by Linamix) - Tatts IRE - September

bc - Tilstarr (by Shamardal) - Goffs - February

bc - Wait Watcher (by Fath) - Goffs - October

HILLSTAR (IRE)

Timeform 121-rated middle-distance Grade 1 scorer has a pedigree that received updates again in 2018 and may do so again this year thanks to the exploits of his half-brother Crystal Ocean (by Sea The Stars). That classic-placed Group 2 star achieved a peak 132 rating from Timeform, finished the year on 129, and could still get compensation for his Group 1 defeats.

Their half-sister Crystal Capella (by Cape Cross), a dual winner of the Group 2 Pride Stakes at Newmarket, put up her most impressive performance when running out an eight-length winner of the Group 2 Princess of Wales's Stakes at the July Course, and their siblings also include the 10-furlong listed scorer Crystal Zvezda (by Dubawi).

Their dam, Crystal Star (by Mark Of Esteem), won the seven-furlong Listed Radley Stakes at two and was Group 3-placed over the same trip at three, and that half-sister to pattern-placed 12-furlong stakes winner Waila (by Notnowcato) is out of Crystal Cavern (by Be My Guest), a winning half-sister to Group 1 Poule d'Essai des Pouliches (French 1000 Guineas) heroine Rose Gypsy (by Green Desert).

This is a prolific blacktype family whose branches and generations also feature the top-level winners Sasuru (by Most Welcome) and Tuscan Evening (by Oasis Dream), and all of this makes Hillstar one of the best-bred young National Hunt stallions at stud. He stands at Garryrichard Stud, which has a long history of producing leading National Hunt stallions, and there were 45 foals in his first crop.

SUMMARY DETAILS

Stood in 2016: Garryrichard Stud, Ireland
Fee in 2016: on application
Career highlights: 4 wins inc Canadian International Stakes (Gr1), King Edward VII Stakes (Gr2), Dubai Duty Free Legacy (Arc Trial) Stakes (Gr3), 2nd Hardwicke Stakes (Gr2), Princess of Wales's Stakes (Gr2), Rose of Lancaster Stakes (Gr3), Ormonde Stakes (Gr3), 3rd King George VI and Queen Elizabeth Stakes (Gr1), Cumberland Lodge Stakes (Gr3)
Standing in 2019: Garryrichard Stud, Ireland
Fee in 2019: on application

Stallions by his sire include: Air Chief Marshal (Gr1), Choisir (Gr1), Fast Company (Gr1), Lizard Island (Gr1), Mastercraftsman (Gr1), Monsieur Bond (Gr1), Silent Times (Gr1), Indesatchel (Gr2), Jeremy (Gr2), Alfred Nobel (Gr3), Planteur (L), Where Or When (L), Hillstar (2yo), Sumbal (new)

HILLSTAR (IRE) – bay 2010

Danehill Dancer (IRE)	Danehill (USA)	Danzig (USA)
		Razyana (USA)
	Mira Adonde (USA)	Sharpen Up
		Lettre D'Amour (USA)
Crystal Star (GB)	Mark Of Esteem (IRE)	Darshaan
		Homage (GB)
	Crystal Cavern (USA)	Be My Guest (USA)
		Krisalya

SALES YEARLINGS OF 2018

Sold in Euros

bc - Spartan Angel (by Beneficial) - Tatts IRE - February - €23,000
bc - Definite Grey (by Sagamix) - Tatts IRE - February - €7,000
bc - Augusta Lucinda (by Luso) - Goffs - February - €5,500
chc - Fair Astronomer (by Persian Mews) - Tatts IRE - February - €5,000
bc - Maritana (by Rahy) - Goffs - November - €3,000

Not Sold

bg - Barton Leader (by Supreme Leader) - Goresbridge - October
chc - Curzon Ridge (by Indian Ridge) - Tatts IRE - February

HOT STREAK (IRE)

Hot Streak is a fascinating member of this cohort of stallions and has the potential to become one of its more successful ones. A high-class sprinter at two and three years of age, and pattern-placed at four, his top Timeform rating was the 120 he got as a juvenile, he is a son of a leading international stallion from the Gone West (by Mr Prospector) line, and comes from a family that has produced several stallions of note.

He is the best of several winners out of Ashirah (by Housebuster) and that unraced half-sister to the Grade 1-placed US Grade 3 scorer Mustanfar (by Unbridled), and to dual English listed scorer Tadris (by Red Ransom), it out of Manwah (by Lyphard), a daughter of Height Of Fashion (by Bustino). That Group 2 Princess of Wales's Stakes heroine was out of the classic star Highclere (by Queen's Hussar) and was the dam of Nayef (by Gulch), Nashwan (by Blushing Groom), and Unfuwain (by Northern Dancer), among others of note. Each of that trio was a top-class racehorse, and each went on to sire Group 1 winners.

Their siblings include Sarayir (by Mr Prospector), who is the stakes-winning dam of the classic-winning miler Ghanaati (by Giant's Causeway), and the many other notable descendants of Height Of Fashion include Grade 1 Breeders' Cup Filly & Mare Turf star Lahudood (by Singspiel), Argentine Grade 1 scorer Il Fornaio (by Orpen), and classic-placed Group 2 Queen Mary Stakes winner Maqaasid (by Green Desert).

Tweenhills Farm & Stud team member Hot Streak had 76 foals in his first crop and looks likely to get talented two-year-olds plus those who do well in the broad five-to-10-furlong range as three-year-olds and older horses. It would be no surprise to see him get at least one or two Group 1 winners among a selection of other stakes winners and high-class handicappers.

SUMMARY DETAILS

Stood in 2016: Tweenhills Farm & Stud, England
Fee in 2016: £7,000
Career highlights: 4 wins inc Temple Stakes (Gr2), Cornwallis Stakes (Gr3), Roses Stakes (L), 2nd Middle Park Stakes (Gr1), 3rd King's Stand Stakes (Gr1), Mill Reef Stakes (Gr2), Palace House Stakes (Gr3), Prix de Saint-Georges (Gr3)

Standing in 2019: Tweenhills Farm & Stud, England
Fee in 2019: £7,000
Stallions by his sire include: Wootton Bassett (Gr1), Benvenue (2yo), Hot Streak (2yo), Biraaj (yearlings), Turn Me Loose (yearlings), Ribchester (foals), Jungle Cat (new)

HOT STREAK (IRE) – chestnut 2011

Iffraaj (GB)	Zafonic (USA)	Gone West (USA)
		Zaizafon (USA)
	Pastorale (GB)	Nureyev (USA)
		Park Appeal
Ashirah (USA)	Housebuster (USA)	Mt Livermore (USA)
		Big Dreams (USA)
	Manwah (USA)	Lyphard (USA)
		Height Of Fashion (FR)

SALES YEARLINGS OF 2018

Sold in Euros

	chf - Stroll Patrol (by Mount Nelson) - Goffs - October - €100,000
Between Hills (IRE)	bf - Breedj (by Acclamation) - Goffs - October - €88,000
Hot Heels (GB)	chc - Poulaine Bleue (by Bertolini) - Tatts IRE - September - €27,000 (p/s)
	bf - Rate (by Galileo) - Tatts IRE - September - €26,000
	bc - Perfect Act (by Act One) - Tatts IRE - September - €18,000
	chf - Maid In Heaven (by Clodovil) - Tatts IRE - September - €16,000
	bc - Billie Eria (by Tamayuz) - Goffs - October - €11,000
	bc - Sleep Dance (by Sleeping Indian) - Tatts IRE - September - €10,000
	bc - Heliograph (by Ishiguru) - Tatts IRE - September - €7,000
	bf - Darwell (by Zamindar) - Tatts IRE - September - €3,500
Laurel Wreath (GB)	chf - Crown (by Royal Applause) - Goresbridge - October - €3,000

Ballyare (GB)   bc - Saddlers Bend (by Refuse To Bend)
                                 - Tatts IRE - September - €1,650 (p/s)

Sold in Guineas

                                 chc - Bossanova Lady (by Street Boss) -
                                 Tattersalls - October - 220,000gns
                                 chc - Bahamamia (by Vettori) -
                                 Tattersalls - October - 200,000gns
                                 chc - Never In (by Elusive City) -
                                 Tattersalls - October - 200,000gns
Albukhturi (GB)   bc - Poyle Dee Dee (by Oasis Dream) -
                                 Tattersalls - October - 150,000gns
Street Life (GB)   chc - Atheera (by Shamardal) -
                                 Tattersalls - October - 62,000gns
Tom Tulliver (GB)   bc - Belle Isle (by Pastoral Pursuits) -
                                 Tattersalls - October - 45,000gns
Leoch (GB)   chc - Acquiesced (by Refuse To Bend) -
                                 Tattersalls - October - 42,000gns
                                 bc - Rose Ransom (by Oasis Dream) -
                                 Tattersalls - October - 40,000gns
Beat The Heat (GB)   bc - Touriga (by Cape Cross) -
                                 Tattersalls - October - 30,000gns
                                 chc - Bestfootforward (by Motivator) -
                                 Tattersalls - October - 27,000gns
                                 chc - Hanella (by Galileo) - Tattersalls -
                                 October - 24,000gns
                                 chc - Royal Sister Two (by Teofilo) -
                                 Tattersalls - November - 18,000gns
                                 chf - Vintage Steps (by Bahamian
                                 Bounty) - Tattersalls - October -
                                 18,000gns
Ho Leng Lui (GB)   bf - Sparkling Eyes (by Lujain) -
                                 Tattersalls - October - 14,000gns
Hot Date (GB)   bf - Speed Date (by Sakhee's Secret) -
                                 Tattersalls - October - 5,000gns

Sold in Pounds

                                 bc - Irishstone (by Danehill Dancer) -
                                 Goffs UK - August - £105,000

bc - Lady Suesanne (by Cape Cross) -
Goffs UK - August - £80,000

Hot Summer (GB)

bc - Lahqa (by Tamayuz) - Goffs UK -
August - £62,000

bf - Acid (by Clodovil) - Goffs UK -
August - £42,000

bc - Talqaa (by Exceed And Excel) -
Goffs UK - August - £40,000

roc - Acquaint (by Verglas) - Goffs UK
- August - £37,000

bc - Enchanted Princess (by Royal
Applause) - Goffs UK - August -
£32,000

bf - Dora's Sister (by Dark Angel) -
Goffs UK - August - £30,000

bc - Park Law (by Fasliyev) - Goffs UK
- August - £28,000

bc - Dangerous Moonlite (by
Acclamation) - Goffs UK - August -
£24,000

bc - Midnight Flower (by Haafhd) -
Goffs UK - August - £20,000

bf - Qatar Princess (by Marju) - Tatts
IRE Ascot - September - £20,000

chf - Vivid Blue (by Haafhd) - Goffs
UK - August - £20,000

chf - Liberty Lady (by Statue Of
Liberty) - Goffs UK - August - £19,000

bc - Dream Of Wunders (by Cape
Cross) - Goffs UK - August - £18,000

bf - Joshua's Princess (by Danehill) -
Goffs UK - August - £18,000

chc - Abbakova (by Dandy Man) - Tatts
IRE Ascot - September - £17,000

Catherine Bay (GB)

bf - Respondez (by Oasis Dream) -
Goffs UK - August - £16,000

bc - Rohesia (by High Chaparral) -
Goffs UK - August - £16,000

chc - Positivity (by Monsieur Bond) -
Tatts IRE Ascot - September - £15,000

bc - Shannon Spree (by Royal Applause)
- Tatts IRE Ascot - September -
£12,500
chc - A Great Beauty (by Acclamation) -
Goffs UK - October - £10,000
bf - Tell The Wind (by Mujadil) - Goffs
UK - August - £10,000 (p/s)
chf - Columella (by Kyllachy) - Tatts
IRE Ascot - September - £3,000
chf - Sunburnt (by Haafhd) - Tatts IRE
Ascot - September - £2,000

Not Sold (inc. vendor buy-backs)

chf - Acts Of Folly (by King's Best) -
Tattersalls - October
chc - Birch Cove (by Shamardal) - Tatts
IRE Ascot - September
chc - Lomapamar (by Nashwan) -
Tattersalls - October
chf - Magic Colour (by Awesome
Again) - Goffs - February

Macstreak (GB)   chc - No Song (by Zamindar) - Tatts
IRE Ascot - December
bf - Royal Obsession (by Val Royal) -
Tattersalls - October
chc - Royal Sister Two (by Teofilo) -
Goffs - October
chf - Signoret (by Naaqoos) - Arqana -
August
chf - Stagecoach Jade (by Peintre
Celebre) - Tatts IRE - September
bf - Steal The Curtain (by Royal
Applause) - Tattersalls - October
bc - Tut (by Intikhab) - Tatts IRE -
September

HUNTER'S LIGHT (IRE)

Triple Group 1 star Hunter's Light is a son of leading international sire Dubawi (by Dubai Millennium), a prolific sire of top-level winners who is awaiting a first significant stallion son. Yes, both Makfi (26 stakes winners including four Group 1 stars) and the late Poet's Voice (sire of 16 stakes winners including Poet's Word and Trap For Fools) have got top-level winners, but their overall records are merely useful. Of course, many of the best of Dubawi's racing sons have yet to have any runners, so there is still every reason to hope that he will come up with at least two or three major sons who will carry on his name.

Those highly-ranked sons include Haras du Logis team member Hunter's Light, whom Timeform rated 126. He was prolific, won or was placed in blacktype events in Dubai, England, Scotland, France, Germany, Italy, and Turkey, and earned over £900,000 in prize money. There were 65 foals in his first crop.

He also has the potential to get some high-class progeny as he is out of Portmanteau (by Barathea), a winning half-sister to the Grade 1-placed Group 2 Grand Prix de Deauville scorer Courteous (by Generous) and out of an unraced full-sister to classic star and influential stallion Darshaan (by Shirley Heights). That also makes his grandam Dayanata a half-sister to the Group 1-placed Group 2 Prix de Royallieu winner Dalara (by Doyoun) – who is the dam of Derby-placed Group 1 Coronation Cup and Group 1 Hong Kong Vase scorer Daliapour (by Sadler's Wells) – and to Group 1 Prix Vermeille heroine and 'blue hen' mare Darara (by Top Ville).

Her four Group 1 stars are Darazari (by Sadler's Wells), Diaghilev/River Dancer (by Sadler's Wells), ill-fated Rewilding (by Tiger Hill), and Dar Re Mi (by Singspiel). The latter, who completed a top-level treble of Pretty Polly Stakes, Yorkshire Oaks, and Dubai Sheema Classic, is now a broodmare of note, and is the dam of the Group 1-placed pattern winner So Mi Dar (by Dubawi), last year's Group 1 St Leger runner-up Lah Ti Dar (by Dubawi), and rising star Too Darn Hot (by Dubawi). The latter was Europe's two-year-old champion in 2018, in what was a strong year at the top of that division, and he is one of the most exciting three-year-old prospects of recent years.

There are many other talented horses to be found in this famous family, and in addition to some potentially smart late-season juveniles, Hunter's Light looks likely to get his best horses within the classic range of distances, with some staying farther.

SUMMARY DETAILS
Stood in 2016: Haras de Logis, France
Fee in 2016: €4,000
Career highlights: 12 wins inc Jebel Hatta (Gr1), Al Maktoum Challenge R3 (Gr1), Premio Roma (Gr1), Al Maktoum Challenge R2 (Gr2), Rose of Lancaster Stakes (Gr3), Anatolia Trophy (L), Dubai Millennium Stakes (L), Churchill Stakes (L), Foundation Stakes (L), Glasgow Stakes (L), 2nd Prix Dollar (Gr2), 3rd Grosser Dallmayr-Preis Bayerisches Zuchtrennen (Gr1), Brigadier Gerard Stakes (Gr3), Gordon Stakes (Gr3)
Standing in 2019: Haras de Logis, France
Fee in 2019: €4,000
Stallions by his sire include: Makfi (Gr1), Poet's Voice (Gr1), Al Kazeem (L), Akeed Mofeed (winners), Monterosso (winners), Universal (winners), Waldpark (winners), Wilful Default (winners), Worthadd (winners), Hunter's Light (2yo), Night Of Thunder (2yo), Red Dubawi (2yo), Willow Magic (2yo), New Bay (yearlings), Dartmouth (foals), Erupt (foals), Postponed (foals), Time Test (foals), Zarak (foals)

HUNTER'S LIGHT (IRE) – chestnut 2008

Dubawi (IRE)	Dubai Millennium (GB)	Seeking The Gold (USA)
		Colorado Dancer
	Zomaradah (GB)	Deploy
		Jawaher (IRE)
Portmanteau (GB)	Barathea (IRE)	Sadler's Wells (USA)
		Brocade
	Dayanata	Shirley Heights
		Delsy (FR)

SALES YEARLINGS OF 2018
Sold in Euros
Secrets De Famille (FR) chf - Louisa M Alcott (by King's Best) - Arqana - October - €38,000
bc - Shinabaa (by Anabaa) - Osarus - September - €21,000

Padirac (FR)	bc - Polyquest (by Poliglote) - Arqana - November - €14,000
Galidermes (FR)	bc - Angie Eria (by Galileo) - Osarus - September - €12,000
	chc - Saga Boreale (by Arch) - Osarus - September - €12,000
	bf - Sugar Loaf (by Singspiel) - Baden-Baden - August - €12,000
	bc - Decency (by Celtic Swing) - Arqana - November - €11,000
Rip Wendy (IRE)	bf - Miss Avonbridge (by Avonbridge) - Arqana - August - €10,000 (p/s)
Six One (FR)	grc - Silky Steps (by Nayef) - Arqana - November - €10,000 (p/s)
Marateca (FR)	chf - Talwin (by Alhaarth) - Osarus - September - €10,000
Lilas Grine (FR)	chf - Unmatched (by Champs Elysees) - Osarus - September - €10,000
Adamina (FR)	bf - Arsila (by Tirol) - Arqana - February - €8,500
Star's Light (FR)	chc - Star Zita (by Starborough) - Arqana - November - €6,500
	chc - Antrim Rose (by Giant's Causeway) - Osarus - September - €6,000
	bc - Rivabella (by Iron Mask) - Arqana - February - €6,000
Mica Malpic (FR)	chc - Moon Malpic (by Green Tune) - Arqana - February - €5,000
Adamina (FR)	bf - Arsila (by Tirol) - Osarus - September - €4,000 (p/s)
Conil Andalucia (FR)	bf - Corn Maiden (by Refuse To Bend) - Arqana - February - €4,500
	bf - Jezlay (by Layman) - BBAG - October - €3,500
Bamm'm De Fontaine (FR)	grc - Lace Ribbons (by Montmartre) - Arqana - November - €2,000

HUNTER'S LIGHT (IRE)

Sold in Guineas

bc - Lady McKell (by Raven's Pass) -
Tattersalls - October - 52,000gns
chf - Corniche (by Manduro) -
Tattersalls - October - 1,000gns

Sold in Pounds

chf - Wild Surmise (by High Chaparral)
- Goffs UK - October - £800

Not Sold (inc. vendor buy-backs)

bc - Blue Lullaby (by Fasliyev) - Arqana
- November

Conil Andalucia (FR)   bf - Corn Maiden (by Refuse To Bend) -
BBAG - October

chf - Pasba (by Danehill Dancer) -
Osarus - September

bf - Polysheba (by Poliglote) - Arqana -
November

Sporting Hunter (GER)   chc - Sugar Babe (by Noroit) - BBAG -
October

Bay Watching (GB)   chf - Tropicana Bay (by Oasis Dream) -
Tattersalls - October

La Korrigane (FR)   chf - Wunschkonzert (by Westerner) -
BBAG - October

FRESHMAN SIRES OF 2019

INTRINSIC (GB)

With only 24 in his first crop, Intrinsic faces an uphill battle to become a sire of note, but this Hedgeholme Stud resident is related to a 2018 freshman stallion who got two pattern winners among his first juveniles, and if he does get any stakes and pattern winners then he certainly won't be the first non-blacktype scorer to do so.

He was rated 114 by Timeform – as was his Group 1-placed, pattern winning dam Infallible (by Pivotal) – he was a lightly-raced winner of the Stewards' Cup, and his best offspring are likely to be sprinters and milers. He is a half-brother to Group 3 Prix de Flore scorer Intimation (by Dubawi) and to multiple Group 1-placed, dual Group 2 Summer Mile Stakes winner Mutakayyef (by Sea The Stars), whereas his dam's siblings include Penchant (by Kyllachy), who is the dam of the Group 1-winning sprinter Garswood (by Dutch Art). That horse stands at Cheveley Park Stud, his Karl Burke-trained daughter Little Kim won the Group 3 Prix du Bois last July and the Frederic Rossi-trained filly Cala Tarida landed the Group 3 Prix de Reservoirs over a mile in late October.

Irresistible (by Cadeaux Genereux), the grandam of Intrinsic, won the Listed Kilvington Stakes and was runner-up in the Group 3 Brownstown Stakes, and that mare is a half-sister to several blacktype producers. Those talented relations include the Group 3 Prix du Calvados winner and Group 2 Criterium de Maisons-Laffitte runner-up Queen Bee (by Le Havre), dual pattern-placed stakes winner Eternally (by Dutch Art), and the colts Parliament Square (by Acclamation) and True Mason (by Mayson), both of whom have finished third in the Group 1 Prix Morny.

If you go back another generation then you find that the fourth dam of Intrinsic is the standout US filly Some Romance (by Fappiano), a winner of both the Grade 1 Frizette Stakes and Grade 1 Matron Stakes and whose blacktype placings included the Grade 1 Santa Anita Oaks, Grade 1 Monmouth Oaks, and Grade 1 Las Virgenes Stakes. That star's descendants also include her great-granddaughter Dona Bruja (by Storm Embrujado), an Argentine Grade 1 winner who has twice been Grade 1-placed in the USA. The first of those was a half-length second to Dacita in the Beverly D Stakes at Arlington in 2017 and the second one was a head loss to A Raving Beauty in the First Lady Stakes over a mile at Keeneland last October.

Intrinsic will have a small number of representatives, in his early years at least, but it would not be a surprise to see a few talented handicappers emerge from among them, and possibly even a blacktype earner or two. Some may win at two, but his best results are likely to come with three-year-olds and older horses.

SUMMARY DETAILS

Stood in 2016: Hedgeholme Stud, England
Fee in 2016: £1,750
Career highlights: 4 wins inc Stewards' Cup
Standing in 2019: Hedgeholme Stud, England
Fee in 2019: £1,750
Stallions by his sire include: Captain Gerrard (Gr1), Showcasing (Gr1), Querari (Gr1), Aqlaam (Gr2), Power (Gr2), Approve (Gr3), Arcano (Gr3), Frozen Power (L), Coach House (winners), Gale Force Ten (winners), Morpheus (winners), Reply (winners), Sri Putra (winners), Fountain Of Youth (2yo), Intrinsic (2yo), Muhaarar (2yo), Charming Thought (yearlings), Free Port Lux (yearlings), De Treville (foals)

INTRINSIC (GB) – bay 2010

Oasis Dream (GB)	Green Desert (USA)	Danzig (USA)
		Foreign Courier (USA)
	Hope (IRE)	Dancing Brave (USA)
		Bahamian
Infallible (GB)	Pivotal (GB)	Polar Falcon (USA)
		Fearless Revival
	Irresistible (GB)	Cadeaux Genereux
		Polish Romance (USA)

SALES YEARLINGS OF 2018
Sold in Pounds

bc - Danehill Dazzler (by Danehill Dancer) - Goffs UK - October - £6,000
chf - She's So Pretty (by Grand Lodge) - Tatts IRE Ascot - September - £5,000
bf - Cara's Delight (by Fusaichi Pegasus) - Tatts IRE Ascot - September - £2,000

Not Sold

bf - Dutch Girl (by Dutch Art) -
Tattersalls - October
bf - Spring Goddess (by Daggers
Drawn) - Tattersalls - October

IVAWOOD (IRE)

A leading juvenile who went on to be placed in two classics at three, Ivawood (by Zebedee) was Timeform-rated 118 in both his seasons to race, he was a popular new addition to the Coolmore roster at Castlehyde Stud and got 80 foals in his first crop.

His speedy sire, Zebedee, raced only as a two-year-old, his grandsire is leading international sire Invincible Spirit (by Green Desert), and he is the first foal out of Keenes Royale (by Red Ransom), a winning half-sister to Group 2 Royal Lodge Stakes scorer Berkshire (by Mount Nelson). That horse stood for a single season in France before moving to Ireland where he now resides at Kedrah House Stud.

Their dam Kinnaird (by Dr Devious) won the Group 1 Prix de l'Opera, her half-brother Mickdaam (by Dubawi) won the Group 3 Chester Vase, and the variety of stakes winners that you find under the fourth dam include classic-placed dual stakes winner Shifting Power (by Compton Place) and last year's Group 1 Prix de Diane (French Oaks) heroine Laurens (by Siyouni), now a five-time Group 1 star.

This pedigree is that of a horse who was bred to show talent at two and be effective at around a mile at three – which is how he turned out. It seems likely that, depending on what the mares contribute, he will get winners in all age groups, with his best progeny being useful anywhere in the broad five-to-10-furlong range, and a few staying a bit farther. Some will show talent as two-year-olds, but given the distaff side of his family, it is possible his best results may come with three-year-olds and older horses.

SUMMARY DETAILS

Stood in 2016: Castlehyde Stud, Co Cork
Fee in 2016: €9,000
Career highlights: 3 wins inc July Stakes (Gr2), Richmond Stakes (Gr2), 2nd Middle Park Stakes (Gr1), 3rd 2000 Guineas (Gr1), Irish 2000 Guineas (Gr1), Greenham Stakes (Gr3)
Standing in 2019: Castlehyde Stud, Co Cork
Fee in 2019: €5,000
Stallions by his sire include: Ivawood (2yo)

IVAWOOD (IRE)

IVAWOOD (IRE) – bay 2012

Zebedee (GB)	Invincible Spirit (IRE)	Green Desert (USA)
		Rafha
	Cozy Maria (USA)	Cozzene (USA)
		Mariamme (USA)
Keenes Royale (GB)	Red Ransom (USA)	Roberto (USA)
		Arabia (USA)
	Kinnaird (IRE)	Dr Devious (IRE)
		Ribot's Guest (IRE)

SALES YEARLINGS OF 2018

Sold in Euros

Ivan The Great (IRE) bc - Krynica (by Danzig) - Goffs - October - €80,000
bf - Parabola (by Galileo) - Goffs - October - €60,000
bf - Foreplay (by Lujain) - Goffs - October - €42,000

Almendro (IRE) bc - Perfect Blossom (by One Cool Cat) - Tatts IRE - September - €40,000
bc - Bridge Note (by Stravinsky) - Tatts IRE - September - €25,000
b/brf - Siesta Time (by Oasis Dream) - Goffs - October - €21,000
bc - Beauthea (by Barathea) - Tatts IRE - September - €20,000

Rusalka (IRE) bf - Song To The Moon (by Oratorio) - Goffs - February - €17,000
bc - Livadiya (by Shernazar) - Goffs - October - €16,000
bc - Theebah (by Bahamian Bounty) - Goffs - October - €16,000
bc - Its In The Air (by Whipper) - Goffs - October - €15,000
bf - Rambert (by Acclamation) - Arqana - August - €15,000 (p/s)
bc - Sandbox Two (by Foxhound) - Tatts IRE - September - €15,000 (p/s)
bc - Selkis (by Darshaan) - Arqana - October - €13,000

131

bc - Rare Tern (by Pivotal) - Goffs - October - €12,000

chc - Free Lance (by Grand Lodge) - Tatts IRE - September - €11,000

bf - Persian Filly (by Persian Bold) - Goffs - February - €11,000

brf - Reign (by Elusive City) - Tatts IRE - September - €9,000

bc - Stormy Larissa (by Royal Applause) - Tatts IRE - September - €7,500

bf - Hearthstead Dancer (by Royal Academy) - Goffs - October - €6,000

bf - Rio's Pearl (by Captain Rio) - Goffs - October - €6,000

bc - Quality Cheryl (by Elusive Quality) - Goffs - November - €4,000 (p/s)

bf - Mafaaza (by Jazil) - Goffs - November - €3,500

bf - Lilly Be (by Titus Livius) - Tatts IRE - September - €3,000

chf - Miss Wicklow (by New Approach) - Goffs - November - €2,000

bf - Caliso Bay (by High Chaparral) - Tatts IRE - September - €1,000

chc - Dream Impossible (by Iffraaj) - Tatts IRE - September - €1,000

bf - Greenflash (by Green Desert) - Goffs - November - €1,000

chc - Rainbow Song (by New Approach) - Goffs - November - €1,000

bf - Takaliyda (by Azamour) - Goffs - November - €1,000

Sold in Guineas

Bryn Du (GB) bc - Caption (by Motivator) - Tattersalls - October - 60,000gns

Itoldyoutobackit (IRE) chc - Jawlaat (by Shamardal) - Tattersalls - October - 60,000gns

bf - Romp (by Pivotal) - Tattersalls - October - 40,000gns

IVAWOOD (IRE)

Love My Life (IRE)	bc - Spring Bouquet (by King's Best) - Tattersalls - October - 38,000gns
	chf - Cradle Brief (by Brief Truce) - Tattersalls - October - 32,000gns
	chc - Highland Miss (by Theatrical) - Tattersalls - October - 2,000gns
	chf - In A Silent Way (by Desert Prince) - Tattersalls - October - 800gns

Sold in Pounds

	bc - Mirror Image (by Acclamation) - Goffs UK - August - £40,000
Lexington Quest (IRE)	bc - Serenata (by Oratorio) - Goffs UK - August - £32,000
Sword Beach (IRE)	chc - Sleeping Princess (by Dalakhani) - Goffs UK - August - £30,000
	brc - Just Joey (by Averti) - Goffs UK - August - £24,000
Alabama Whitman (GB)	bf - Mutoon (by Erhaab) - Goffs UK - August - £18,000
War Of Clans (IRE)	bc - Precautionary (by Green Desert) - Goffs UK - August - £18,000 (p/s)
	bc - Angelic Angie (by Approve) - Goffs UK - August - £9,000
	chf - Dancing With Stars (by Where Or When) - Goffs UK - August - £9,000
Komorebi (GB)	chf - Spangle (by Galileo) - Goffs UK - August - £9,000
	chf - Much Faster (by Fasliyev) - Tatts IRE Ascot - September - £8,000
Iva Go (IRE)	bf - Enliven (by Dansili) - Goffs UK - August - £4,000

Not Sold (inc. vendor buy-backs)

	bf - Absolute Pleasure (by Polar Falcon) - Goffs - November
	chc - Alexander Divine (by Halling) - Goffs - February
	bc - Amarylis (by Rip Van Winkle) - Tatts IRE Ascot - September

bf - Annacurra (by Verglas) - Goffs -
February

bf - Annacurra (by Verglas) - Goffs UK
- August

bf - Beseech (by Danehill) - Goffs -
November

chg - Bond's Girl (by Monsieur Bond) -
Tattersalls - October

bf - Caperina (by Cape Cross) - Goffs -
November

bf - Ceoldrama (by Mr Greeley) - Goffs
- November

bc - Coco Demure (by Titus Livius) -
Arqana - August

brf - Cute Cait (by Atraf) - Tatts IRE -
September

Ivy Avenue (IRE)   chf - Dance Avenue (by Sadler's Wells)
- Tatts IRE - September

bf - Delitme (by Val Royal) - Goffs -
November

chf - Duchess Diva (by Duke Of
Marmalade) - Goffs - February

bf - Impressive Victory (by Street Cry) -
Tatts IRE - September

bc - Jesting (by Muhtarram) - Tatts IRE
- September

bc - Khyber Knight (by Night Shift) -
Goffs UK - August

bc - Lady Berta (by Bertolini) - Tatts
IRE - September

bf - Lalinde (by Tiger Hill) - Tatts IRE -
September

bc - Last Gold (by Gold Away) -
Arqana - August

bc - Last Gold (by Gold Away) -
Tattersalls - November

bc - Lilakiya (by Dr Fong) - Goffs -
November

bf - Musical Peace (by Oratorio) - Tatts
IRE - September

bf - Pearl Blue (by Exceed And Excel) -
Goffs - November
bf - Picture Of Lily (by Medicean) -
Tattersalls - October
bc - Real Magic (by Pour Moi) -
Tattersalls - October
bf - Seeking Dubai (by Dubawi) - Tatts
IRE - September
bc - Sharp Applause (by Royal
Applause) - Tatts IRE - September

Rusalka (IRE)
bf - Song To The Moon (by Oratorio) -
Goffs UK - August
bc - Woodsophiesmile (by Acclamation)
- Tatts IRE - September

KARAKONTIE (JPN)

Bernstein (by Storm Cat) looked like a potential Group 1 star in the making following two early-season juvenile wins that were achieved by a combined margin of 10 lengths. First was a maiden in late May, the second was the Group 3 Railway Stakes, and both were over six furlongs on good ground at the Curragh. He was sent off a 4/11 favourite for the Group 1 National Stakes over a quarter-mile farther at the same venue three months later but failed to make the frame as subsequent Arc and dual Derby hero Sinndar landed the spoils. He won two of his five starts at three, including the Group 3 Coolmore Stud Home of Champions Concorde Stakes over seven furlongs on soft ground at Cork, and was retired to stand at Buck Pond Farm in Kentucky.

He moved to Castleton Lyons Stud four years later, he shuttled to Argentina, and he became a prolific blacktype sire. Many associate him immediately with his brilliant daughter Tepin, but his top performers also feature Karakontie. The Niarchos Family-bred colt was born in Japan but trained by Jonathan Pease in France where he was a top-class performer at two and three years of age.

Although touched off in a seven-furlong listed contest at Deauville on his second start, he stepped up on that form to take both the Group 3 Prix La Rochette and Group 1 Prix Jean-Luc Lagardere, thereby establishing himself as the top juvenile colt in France, one of the best of his age in Europe, and a leading classic prospect for 2014. He duly won the Group 1 Poule d'Essai des Poulains (French 2000 Guineas) the following spring, and although disappointing in the Prix du Jockey-Club (French Derby) and Prix de la Foret, he rounded off that campaign with a one-length defeat of Anodin in the Grade 1 Breeders' Cup Mile at Santa Anita.

Karakontie remained in training as a four-year-old but ran just three times, with his two-length third to Ervedya in the Group 1 Prix du Moulin de Longchamp the standout performance. He retired to Gainesway in Kentucky, yearlings from his first crop found buyers at all levels of the market, and he is an intriguing stallion prospect, especially as he is related to an influential Group 1 sire.

The best of several winners out of Sun Is Up (by Sunday Silence), this half-brother to mile listed scorer Bottega (by Mineshaft) is out of a half-sister to Amanee (by Pivotal), who was a one-mile Grade 1 winner in South Africa. The mare's dam Moon Is Up (by Woodman) won a listed contest over that same trip at Deauville shortly before taking third place to Kistena in the Group 3 Prix de Seine-et-Oise over six furlongs at Maisons-Laffitte – talented form but a long way behind what the best of her siblings achieved. That's because Moon Is Up is a daughter of the great Miesque (by Nureyev), one of the most brilliant filly milers of all time and a broodmare of considerable influence.

Her star son Kingmambo (by Mr Prospector) was a classic-winning triple Group 1 star and later a leading international sire, her top daughter is the dual French classic heroine East Of The Moon (by Private Account), and she was also responsible for the pattern-winning colts Miesque's Son (by Mr Prospector) and Mingun (by A.P. Indy). Miesque's other notable descendants include last year's European classic stars Alpha Centauri (by Mastercraftsman) and Study Of Man (by Deep Impact).

With racing and pedigree credentials like these, plus how his first yearlings fared in the auction ring, there is every reason to hope that Karakontie can do well as a stallion. He should get winners in all age groups, his best winners could come anywhere in the five-to-10-furlong range – with a chance of some staying a bit farther – and it would not be a surprise to see him get winners at all levels, including some who can succeed in Group/Grade 1 contests.

SUMMARY DETAILS

Stood in 2016: Gainesway, Kentucky, USA
Fee in 2016: $15,000
Career highlights: 5 wins inc Breeders' Cup Mile (Gr1), Poule d'Essai des Poulains (Gr1), Qatar Prix Jean-Luc Lagardere (Gr1), Prix La Rochette (Gr3), 2nd Prix de Fontainebleau (Gr3), Prix François Boutin (L), 3rd Qatar Prix du Moulin de Longchamp (Gr1)
Standing in 2019: Gainesway, Kentucky, USA
Fee in 2019: $10,000

Stallions by his sire include: Storm Embrujado (Gr1),
Goshawk Ken (Gr3), Tan Chemistry (Gr3), Signature Red (L),
Karakontie (2yo)

KARAKONTIE (JPN) – bay 2011

		Storm Bird (CAN)
Bernstein (USA)	Storm Cat (USA)	Storm Bird (CAN)
		Terlingua (USA)
	La Affirmed (USA)	Affirmed (USA)
		La Mesa (USA)
Sun Is Up (JPN)	Sunday Silence (USA)	Halo (USA)
		Wishing Well (USA)
	Moon Is Up (USA)	Woodman (USA)
		Miesque (USA)

SALES YEARLINGS OF 2018

Sold in Euros

Ketil (USA) — c - Matroshka (by Red Ransom) - Arqana - August - €50,000
f - Linnea Cal (by Crafty Prospector) - Goffs - October - €35,000
c - Janine's Approval (by Approve) - Arqana - October - €32,000

Karafria (GB) — f - Aguafria (by More Than Ready) - Arqana - October - €5,000

Sold in Guineas

Glenties (USA) — c - Candy Kitty (by Lemon Drop Kid) - Tattersalls - October - 52,000gns

Sold in US Dollars

c - Judy In Disguise (by Elusive City) - Keeneland - September - $220,000
f - Oblivious (by Cozzene) - Keeneland - September - $150,000
c - Afleet Lass (by Northern Afleet) - Keeneland - September - $130,000
c - Athehsa (by Big Brown) - Keeneland - September - $125,000
c - Cruise (by Posse) - Keeneland - September - $120,000

Karakontie Flyer (USA) f - Pretty City (by Carson City) - Keeneland - September - $120,000
c - I Bet Toni Knows (by Sunriver) - Keeneland - September - $100,000
f - Sassifaction (by Smart Strike) - Keeneland - September - $75,000
f - Graceful Grit (by Holy Roman Emperor) - Keeneland - September - $65,000
f - Transact (by Hard Spun) - Fasig-Tipton Kentucky - October - $65,000
f - Unobstructed View (by Yes It's True) - Keeneland - September - $50,000
f - Jaded Glory (by Smart Strike) - Keeneland - September - $37,000
c - Talented Tap (by Tapit) - Keeneland - January - $35,000
f - Church Camp (by Forest Camp) - Keeneland - September - $30,000
f - Hope Bay (by Smart Strike) - Fasig-Tipton Kentucky - October - $30,000
c - Jera (by Jeblar) - Keeneland - September - $30,000
c - Spanish Bunny (by Unusual Heat) - Keeneland - September - $25,000
c - Talented Tap (by Tapit) - Fasig-Tipton Kentucky - October - $25,000
c - Unspoken Fur (by Empire Maker) - Keeneland - September - $23,000
f - Southbound (by Southern Image) - Keeneland - September - $22,000
c - She's Striking (by Smart Strike) - Barretts - October - $17,000
f - Spring Free (by Royal Academy) - Keeneland - September - $17,000
c - Friend Of A Friend (by Crafty Friend) - Keeneland - September - $16,000

f - Street Savy (by Street Sense) - Ocala Breeders' Sales Company - October - $16,000

c - Aint She A Saint (by Saintly Look) - Keeneland - September - $15,000

f - Calendar Girl (by Elusive Quality) - Keeneland - September - $10,000

c - Lateen (by Henrythenavigator) - Keeneland - September - $10,000

c - Meadowlanding (by Meadowlake) - Keeneland - September - $10,000

c - Volver (by Danehill Dancer) - Keeneland - September - $10,000

f - Communion (by Pulpit) - Keeneland - September - $8,000

f - Lady Pewitt (by Orientate) - Keeneland - September - $8,000

c - Perelli (by Colonel John) - Fasig-Tipton Kentucky - October - $7,500

f - Magic Of Reality (by Galileo) - Keeneland - September - $7,000

f - Violet Hour (by Elusive Quality) - Keeneland - September - $6,500

f - Andover The Cast (by Unusual Heat) - Keeneland - September - $6,000

c - Lemon Sakhee (by Lemon Drop Kid) - Keeneland - September - $6,000

c - Light Blow (by Kingmambo) - Keeneland - September - $6,000

c - Timeless Spirit (by Devil His Due) - Fasig-Tipton Kentucky - October - $6,000

f - Lemon Hero (by Lemon Drop Kid) - Keeneland - September - $5,500

c - Spring Season (by Seeking The Gold) - Keeneland - January - $5,500

c - Modesty Blaise (by A.P. Indy) - Keeneland - September - $5,000

f - Street Savy (by Street Sense) - Keeneland - January - $5,000

140

c - Cocktail Hour (by Dynaformer) - Fasig-Tipton Midlantic - October - $4,000

Causeway Chrome (USA) f - Broad Causeway (by Giant's Causeway) - Fasig-Tipton Kentucky - October - $3,500
c - Homestake (by Afleet Alex) - Fasig-Tipton Kentucky - October - $3,500
f - Rag And Bone (by Street Cry) - Fasig-Tipton Kentucky - February - $1,500
c - Homestake (by Afleet Alex) - Fasig-Tipton Kentucky - February - $1,000

Not Sold (inc. vendor buy-backs)

c - Aljariah (by Sahm) - Keeneland - September
c - Beach (by Tapit) - Fasig-Tipton New York - August
c - Capaz (by Bernardini) - Barretts - October
f - Coya (by Deputy Minister) - Keeneland - September
c - Credible (by Dixieland Band) - Barretts - October
f - Down The Well (by Mujadil) - Keeneland - September
f - If Not For Lust (by Not For Love) - Fasig-Tipton Kentucky - October
f - Lemon Hero (by Lemon Drop Kid) - Keeneland - January
c - Manaahil (by Mr Greeley) - Keeneland - September
c - Miss Frost (by Curlin) - Fasig-Tipton New York - August
c - Sobinka (by Sadler's Wells) - Keeneland - September
f - Twinkler (by Benny The Dip) - Keeneland - September

FRESHMAN SIRES OF 2019

f - Viva Allegiance (by Proud Citizen) -
Keeneland - September

KINGSTON HILL (GB)

Unbeaten in three starts as a late-season juvenile, Kingston Hill went on to become a leading middle-distance performer at three, chasing home Australia in the Derby at Epsom, winning the St Leger at Doncaster, and finishing fourth in both the Group 1 Coral-Eclipse Stakes and Group 1 Prix de l'Arc de Triomphe. Timeform rated him 119p at two and 125 for his second season. He is a member of the Coolmore stallion team, stands at their Castlehyde Stud, and there were 78 foals in his first crop.

He is a first-crop son of classic and multiple top-level winner Mastercraftsman (by Danehill Dancer) and so is by the sire of classic stars The Grey Gatsby (sire in France) and Alpha Centauri, among an overall total of a dozen Group 1 stars among 58 individual stakes winners, and counting.

Kingston Hill is the best representative of Group 3 Prix de Flore scorer Audacieuse (by Rainbow Quest), his dam's siblings include Group 3 Acomb Stakes winner Waiter's Dream (by Oasis Dream) and pattern-placed, stakes-winning stayer Lord Jim (by Kahyasi), and his grandam is a half-sister to a classic winner. That star is Group 1 Poule d'Essai des Pouliches (French 1000 Guineas) and Group 1 Prix de la Foret heroine Danseuse Du Soir (by Thatching), who is the dam of Group 1 Gran Criterium scorer Scintillo (by Fantastic Light) and of multiple Irish pattern winner Jumbajukiba (by Barathea).

The other blacktype horses under this third generation of the family include Group 2-placed middle-distance stakes winner Don Corleone (by Caerleon), dual listed scorer Dana Springs (by Aragon), Group 1 Prix du Jockey Club third Circus Dance (by Sadler's Wells), and – more distantly connected to those horses – the talented Danzon (by Royal Academy) who was a pattern winner in France before going on to become a Grade 1-placed dual Grade 3 scorer in the USA.

Kingston Hill's pedigree represents a mixture of miler speed with middle-distance stamina, and it seems likely that most of his offspring will prove best as three-year-olds and older horses and in the broad mile-to-two-mile-plus range. He will, of course, get two-year old winners too, although the best of them are likely to be seen out in the second half of the season.

SUMMARY DETAILS

Stood in 2016: Castlehyde Stud, Ireland
Fee in 2016: €6,000
Career highlights: 4 wins inc St Leger Stakes (Gr1), Racing Post Trophy (Gr1), Autumn Stakes (Gr3), 2nd Derby Stakes (Gr1)
Standing in 2019: Castlehyde Stud, Ireland
Fee in 2019: €5,000
Stallions by his sire include: Kingston Hill (2yo), The Grey Gatsby (foals), Master Carpenter (new)

KINGSTON HILL (GB) – grey 2011

Mastercraftsman (IRE)	Danehill Dancer (IRE)	Danehill (USA)
		Mira Adonde (USA)
	Starlight Dreams (USA)	Black Tie Affair
		Reves Celestes (USA)
Audacieuse (GB)	Rainbow Quest (USA)	Blushing Groom (FR)
		I Will Follow (USA)
	Sarah Georgina	Persian Bold
		Dance By Night

SALES YEARLINGS OF 2018

Sold in Euros

Army Of One (GER)	bf - Auctorita (by Authorized) - BBAG - October - €61,000
	bg - Celestial Dream (by Oasis Dream) - Tatts IRE - November - €27,000
	bc - Gwen Lady Byron (by Dandy Man) - Tatts IRE - September - €27,000
	grc - Cattiva Generosa (by Cadeaux Genereux) - Goffs - February - €26,000
La Grace Dieu (FR)	grf - Union Sacree (by Naaqoos) - Osarus - September - €25,000
	b/brc - Beautiful Dreamer (by Red Ransom) - Goffs - November - €23,000
	bc - Ella Watson (by Supreme Leader) - Tatts IRE - February - €21,000
	chc - Senhall (by Halling) - SGA - September - €20,000
Ladyval (FR)	bf - Ladyluve (by Monsun) - Arqana - November - €16,000

KINGSTON HILL (GB)

chf - Ataahua (by Tertullian) - Baden-Baden - August - €15,000

grc - Phantasy Rock (by Rock Of Gibraltar) - Goffs - February - €12,000

grc - Aries Ballerina (by Peintre Celebre) - Goffs - February - €7,000

brc - Iojo (by Giant's Causeway) - Baden-Baden - August - €6,000

bc - Lady Aria Starck (by Aussie Rules) - Goffs - February - €6,000

bc - Sarella Loren (by Theatrical) - Goffs - February - €6,000

bf - Magnificient Bell (by Octagonal) - Goffs - November - €5,200

Dawn Hill (FR)   brf - Delma (by Authorized) - BBAG - October - €4,000

grf - Beal Ban (by Daggers Drawn) - Tatts IRE - September - €7,500

b/grf - Starlight Night (by Distant View) - Tatts IRE - September - €7,000

chf - Supercharged (by Iffraaj) - Tatts IRE - September - €5,000

chc - Redona (by Le Vie Dei Colori) - Tatts IRE - September - €4,000 (p/s)

grf - Biasca (by Erhaab) - Goffs - November - €3,700

chc - Silent Confession (by Mr Greeley) - Goffs - November - €3,200

grf - Lally Mut (by Muhtathir) - Goffs - November - €2,800

chc - Candy Mountain (by Selkirk) - Goffs - November - €2,500

bc - Nagambie (by Duke Of Marmalade) - Goffs - November - €2,200

bf - Liberty Grace (by Statue Of Liberty) - Goffs - November - €2,000

bc - Momma Bear (by Excellent Art) - Goffs - November - €1,000

grf - Rutland Water (by Hawk Wing) -
Goffs - February - €1,000

Sold in Guineas

Sebille (GB)   bf - Inchiri (by Sadler's Wells) -
                            Tattersalls - October - 60,000gns
Hear Me Out (IRE)   bc - Waha (by Oasis Dream) -
                            Tattersalls - October - 40,000gns
                            blc - Shakeeba (by Sendawar) -
                            Tattersalls - November - 18,000gns

Sold in Pounds

                            chc - Adelfia (by Sinndar) - Tatts IRE
                            Ascot - September - £17,000
                            bc - Kinigi (by Verglas) - Goffs UK -
                            August - £9,000 (p/s)
                            chc - Ikan (by Sri Pekan) - Goffs UK -
                            August - £2,000

Not Sold (inc. vendor buy-backs)

                            grg - Cattiva Generosa (by Cadeaux
                            Genereux) - Tatts IRE - November
                            bc - Cigalia (by Red Ransom) - Arqana -
                            November
                            grf - Dress Up (by Noverre) - Goffs -
                            November
                            bc - Good Chocolate (by Fayruz) - Tatts
                            IRE - September
                            bc - Grand Minstrel (by Askhalani) -
                            Tatts IRE - November
Allrigtnow (ITY)   grc - Kermanshah (by Dalakhani) - SGA
                            - September
                            bc - Sarella Loren (by Theatrical) -
                            Goffs - November
                            bc - Sweetly Does It (by Shirocco) -
                            Tattersalls - October
                            bf - Taste Of More (by High Chaparral)
                            - Goffs - February

LUCKY SPEED (IRE)

Sunnyhill Stud stallion Lucky Speed (by Silvano) represents a blending of three of the most influential sire lines in the National Hunt sector, and that makes this Group 1 Deutsches Derby winner a promising prospect. There were 32 foals in his first crop.

He is by the leading South African sire Silvano (by Lomitas), which makes him a representative of the Nijinsky (by Northern Dancer) line, he is out of the pattern-placed 10-furlong winner Lysuna, who is a daughter of the outstanding German stallion Monsun (by Konigsstuhl), and his grandam is a daughter of runaway Derby hero Slip Anchor (by Shirley Heights), a grandson of the mighty Mill Reef (by Never Bend).

Two of his siblings have proven to be notable performers under National Hunt rules, with the Grade 2-placed Lyvius (by Paolini) having won the Listed Gerry Feilden Hurdle and Lyonell (by Montjeu) having taken a two-and-a-half-mile Grade 2 contest over hurdles in the USA. What's more, Lucky Speed also has the attraction of being from the family of a successful stallion as his third dam – La Luna (by Lyphard) – is a winning full-sister to the multiple pattern-winning miler Bellypha, whose stakes-winning offspring include Group 1 Poule d'Essai des Pouliches (French 1000 Guineas) heroine Silvermine, Group 1 Oaks d'Italia winner Lady Bentley, and classic-placed Group 2 scorer Bella Colora, just one of her sire's notable broodmare daughters.

Lucky Speed is unlikely to have more than just the occasional runner on the flat as his future lies as a sire of point-to-pointers and National Hunt horses.

SUMMARY DETAILS

Stood in 2016: Sunnyhill Stud, Ireland
Fee in 2016: on application
Career highlights: 4 wins inc Deutsches Derby (Gr1), Bavarian Classic (Gr3), American St Leger (Gr3), 2nd Fruhjahrs-Preis des Bankhauses Metzler (Gr3), 3rd Grosser Preis von Berlin (Gr1), Grosser Preis der Badischen Unternehmer (Gr2)
Standing in 2019: Sunnyhill Stud, Ireland
Fee in 2019: €1,500

LUCKY SPEED (IRE)

Stallions by his sire include: Bold Silvano (Gr1), Djasil
(winners), Proudinsky (winners), Vercingetorix (winners), Lucky
Speed (2yo)

LUCKY SPEED (IRE) – bay 2010

	Lomitas (GB)	Niniski (USA)
Silvano (GER)		La Colorada (GER)
	Spirit Of Eagles (USA)	Beau's Eagle (USA)
		Big Spirit (USA)
	Monsun (GER)	Konigsstuhl (GER)
Lysuna (GER)		Mosella (GER)
	La Lyra (GB)	Slip Anchor
		La Luna (USA)

SALES YEARLINGS OF 2018
Sold in Euros

bc - La Brave (by Villez) - Tatts IRE -
January - €16,500
chg - Cabra Cruizor (by Swift Gulliver) -
Tatts IRE - November - €10,000

MAKE BELIEVE (GB)

A lightly-raced, Timeform 127-rated classic star who also landed a Group 1 over seven furlongs, Make Believe (by Makfi) was a popular addition to the team at Ballylinch Stud, getting a triple-digit book in his maiden season. With 76 in that first crop, he won't be short of representation.

The grandson of Dubawi (by Dubai Millennium) was a late-season juvenile who ran twice and won on both soft and heavy ground. He lost out by a head in the Group 3 Prix Djebel on his first start at three but then easily beat subsequent classic star New Bay in the Group 1 Poule d'Essai des Poulains (French 2000 Guineas). Later, he beat Limato in the Group 1 Prix de la Foret.

In terms of pedigree, he is something of an unknown prospect as a stallion, and it will be fascinating to see how he turns out. It is true that if you go back far enough then you will find that his fifth dam, Ash Lawn (by Charlottesville), was a full-sister to Selhurst and half-sister to Royal Palace (by Ballymoss), which also means that he represents a branch of the family of Welsh Pageant (by Tudor Melody) and Desert Prince (by Green Desert). Royal Palace, Welsh Pageant and Desert Prince got winners at all levels, but it is fair to say that none became a consistent leading sire. They are, however, only remotely connected to Make Believe, and while their presence does show that a stallion from this family can get stakes, pattern and Group 1 winners, it is possible that their younger relation could surpass their achievements at stud.

He is a three-parts brother to the dual US Grade 1 winner Dubawi Heights (by Dubawi) – who is the dam of Japanese Grade 2 scorer Liberty Heights (by King Kamehameha) – and their dam, Rosie's Posy (by Suave Dancer), is a winning half-sister to Group 1 Sprint Cup heroine Tante Rose (by Barathea). That star is the grandam of a Grade 3 scorer in the US, she is a half-sister to pattern-placed stakes winner Bay Tree (by Daylami) and to the dam of Italian Group 3 winner Gothic Dance (by Dalakhani), and she is out of My Branch, who was one of the best runners for her top-class miler sire Distant Relative (by Habitat). My Branch won the Listed Firth of Clyde Stakes at two and was runner-up in the Group 1 Cheveley Park Stakes, she went on to take third in the Group 1 Irish 1000 Guineas and then to win the Listed Sceptre Stakes. The best of her siblings is the Grade 1-

winning hurdler Celestial Halo (by Galileo).

These are the highlights of the first four generations of the pedigree, hence the unknown element of Make Believe's stallion potential. It was a weak branch of the aforementioned famous Joel family of Royal Palace, Welsh Pageant, etc. – and eighth dam Picture Play (by Donatello) won the 1000 Guineas in 1944 – but there is something about the pedigree that catches the eye. Make Believe is inbred 4x4 to Green Valley (by Val De Loir). This may have no impact on how he fares, but it is worth noting that this mare gave us the classic star and influential sire Green Dancer (by Nijinsky) and also Irish Valley (by Irish River), the dam of juvenile champion and classic sire Alhaarth (by Unfuwain).

His pedigree and racing profile suggest that, depending on the mares, he will get his best winners in the broad five to 12-furlong range, with his better juveniles appearing in the latter half of the season. A handful of his first yearlings fetched six-figure sums in the auction ring, with the top price being 210,000gns for the son of an Alhaarth mare in October.

SUMMARY DETAILS

Stood in 2016: Ballylinch Stud, Ireland
Fee in 2016: €20,000
Career highlights: 4 wins inc Poule d'Essai des Poulains (Gr1), Prix de la Foret (Gr1), 2nd Prix Djebel (Gr3)
Standing in 2019: Ballylinch Stud, Ireland
Fee in 2019: €12,000
Stallions by his sire include: Make Believe (2yo)

MAKE BELIEVE (GB) – bay 2012

Makfi (GB)	Dubawi (IRE)	Dubai Millennium (GB)
		Zomaradah (GB)
	Dhelaal (GB)	Green Desert (USA)
		Irish Valley (USA)
Rosie's Posy (IRE)	Suave Dancer (USA)	Green Dancer (USA)
		Suavite (USA)
	My Branch (GB)	Distant Relative
		Pay The Bank

SALES YEARLINGS OF 2018

Sold in Euros

True Scarlet (IRE)   bf - Lady Pimpernel (by Sir Percy) - Arqana - August - €180,000
bf - Laviniad (by Lawman) - Goffs - October - €150,000
bc - Lady Shanghai (by Alhaarth) - Goffs - February - €115,000

Fairy Garden (IRE)   bf - Somoushe (by Black Minnaloushe) - Goffs - October - €115,000
bc - Spontaneous (by Sinndar) - Goffs - October - €90,000
bf - Ezalli (by Cape Cross) - Goffs - October - €75,000

Gin Blossom (IRE)   grf - Queen Of Power (by Medicean) - Goffs - October - €75,000

Imaginary Friend (IRE) bf - Waafiah (by Anabaa) - Goffs - October - €70,000
bf - Newsletter (by Sir Percy) - Tatts IRE - September - €55,000
bc - Expectation (by Night Shift) - Goffs - February - €42,000
bc - Bailonguera (by Southern Halo) - Goffs - October - €38,000
bc - Malea (by Oratorio) - Goffs - October - €35,000
bc - Bound Copy (by Street Cry) - Goffs - February - €32,000
bf - Twiggy's Sister (by Flying Spur) - Goffs - October - €30,000
bc - Expectation (by Night Shift) - Tatts IRE - September - €25,000
bc - Bayja (by Giant's Causeway) - Goffs - October - €22,000
bf - Iuturna (by Intidab) - Goffs - October - €22,000
bf - Mouriyana (by Akarad) - Goffs - October - €20,000
bf - Royal Alchemist (by Kingsinger) - Goffs - October - €20,000

bc - Bound Copy (by Street Cry) - Goffs
- October - €17,000
bf - Royal Razalma (by Lope De Vega) -
Goffs - October - €15,500
bf - Queen Jock (by Repent) - Tatts IRE
- September - €14,000
bc - Manaka (by Falco) - Tatts IRE -
September - €8,000
bf - Follow My Lead (by Night Shift) -
Tatts IRE - September - €7,500
bf - Shirin Of Persia (by Dylan Thomas)
- Goffs - October - €6,500
bf - Miss Bex (by Dalakhani) - Arqana -
October - €5,000 (p/s)
bf - Cruck Realta (by Sixties Icon) -
Tatts IRE - September - €3,000
bf - Water Fountain (by Mark Of
Esteem) - Goffs - November - €1,000

Sold in Guineas

bc - Lady Shanghai (by Alhaarth) -
Tattersalls - October - 210,000gns
Kafee (IRE)   bc - Dream Date (by Oasis Dream) -
Tattersalls - November - 55,000gns
bc - French Fern (by Royal Applause) -
Tattersalls - October - 55,000gns
bf - Topka (by Kahyasi) - Tattersalls -
October - 55,000gns
bf - Elshamms (by Zafonic) - Tattersalls
- October - 42,000gns
bc - Lake Moon (by Tiger Hill) -
Tattersalls - October - 40,000gns
bf - Gilded (by Redback) - Tattersalls -
October - 35,000gns
bf - Night Fever (by Galileo) -
Tattersalls - October - 35,000gns (p/s)
bc - Sound Of Guns (by Acclamation) -
Tattersalls - October - 35,000gns
bf - Lisselan Diva (by Barathea) -
Tattersalls - October - 27,000gns

	bc - Purple Sage (by Danehill Dancer) - Tattersalls - October - 24,000gns
	bc - Mise (by Indian Ridge) - Tattersalls - October - 22,000gns
Low Fell (GB)	bf - Never Change (by New Approach) - Tattersalls - October - 15,000gns
	bf - For Joy (by Singspiel) - Tattersalls - October - 16,000gns
	bc - Levanto (by Lawman) - Tattersalls - October - 9,000gns
	bc - Mary Arnold (by Hernando) - Tattersalls - October - 6,500gns
Russian Rumour (IRE)	bf - Russian Rave (by Danehill Dancer) - Tattersalls - October - 4,000gns
	bf - Pharadelle (by Lope De Vega) - Tattersalls - November - 3,000gns (p/s)

Sold in Pounds

Fantasy Believer (IRE)	bc - Avizare (by Lawman) - Goffs UK - August - £38,000
Girl From Mars (IRE)	f - Miss Lucy Jane (by Aqlaam) - Goffs UK - August - £35,000
Queens Road (IRE)	bf - Okba (by Diesis) - Tatts IRE Ascot - September - £5,500

Not Sold (inc. vendor buy-backs)

	bc - Bailonguera (by Southern Halo) - Goffs - February
	bf - Basira (by Azamour) - Arqana - August
	bf - Elite (by Invincible Spirit) - Tattersalls - October
	bc - Esuvia (by Whipper) - Tattersalls - November
	bf - Famusa (by Medicean) - Tatts IRE Ascot - December
	bc - Kayd Kodaun (by Traditionally) - Tattersalls - October
	bf - Knapton Hill (by Zamindar) - Tattersalls - October

bc - Ocean Bluff (by Dalakhani) -
Tattersalls - November
bc - Purple Tigress (by Dubai
Destination) - Goffs UK - August
bc - Realt Eile (by Dark Angel) -
Tattersalls - October
bf - Roxy Star (by Fastnet Rock) - Goffs
UK - August
bf - Roxy Star (by Fastnet Rock) - Tatts
IRE Ascot - November
bf - Ryninch (by Dr Devious) - Goffs -
October
bc - Sandslide (by King's Best) - Goffs -
October
bc - Slope (by Acclamation) - Tatts IRE
- September
grc - Stella River (by Stormy River) -
Goffs UK - August
bc - Stylish One (by Invincible Spirit) -
Goffs UK - August
bf - Sun City (by Montjeu) - Tatts IRE -
September
bf - Three Choirs (by Rock Of
Gibraltar) - Goffs - October
bf - Zerka (by Invincible Spirit) - Goffs
UK - October

MUHAARAR (GB)

The Group 1 Commonwealth Cup has been one of the best additions to the European racing programme in recent years, and it got off to a tremendous start as Muhaarar won its inaugural edition. Timeform-rated 111 as a juvenile, when he won the Group 2 Gimcrack Stakes and finished third in the Group 1 Middle Park Stakes, the Charles Hills-trained son of Oasis Dream (by Green Desert) kicked off his three-year-old campaign with a narrow win in the Group 3 Greenham Stakes over seven furlongs but then finished out of the frame in the Group 1 Poule d'Essai des Poulains (French 2000 Guineas).

The distaff side of his family and the fact he is inbred 4x5 to Mill Reef (by Never Bend) suggested that the mile could be within his compass, but after this classic defeat, the decision was taken to drop him back in trip. The Commonwealth Cup and enhanced early-season sprint programme give three-year-olds a chance to compete among themselves before being pitched in against the older horses, so the new race became an obvious starting point. He stormed home by three and three-quarter lengths from Limato, and, in addition to the runner-up, the also-rans included the subsequent Group 1 stars Profitable and Jungle Cat. He went on to a short-head success in the Group 1 July Cup, beat Esoterique by half a length to land the Group 1 Prix Maurice de Gheest, and then came home two lengths clear of Twilight Son in the Group 1 British Champions Sprint Stakes at Ascot.

This Group 1 four-timer represented his only starts after his classic defeat, he was crowned sprint champion, earned a Timeform rating of 132, and went to Nunnery Stud as an exciting stallion prospect. His triple-digit first book yielded 95 foals, and his initial sales yearlings were in high demand, a double-digit total of them fetching six-figure sums and a top price of 925,000gns for his half-sister to Group 1 Cheveley Park Stakes winner Fairyland (by Kodiac).

The best of four blacktype horses for his dam, the half-brother to juvenile listed scorer Sajwah (by Exceed And Excel) is out of Tahrir (by Linamix), a dual seven-furlong winner who earned her blacktype when runner-up in a six-furlong listed contest. The mare is a full-sister to pattern-placed multiple stakes winner Mister Charm and half-sister to Group 3 Prix de Guiche scorer and Group 2 Prix Daniel Wildenstein third Mister Sacha (by Tiger Hill), hence her potential to produce a high-class miler.

Grandam Miss Sacha (by Last Tycoon) was a stakes-winning sprinter, a half-sister to the listed scorer Pinta (by Ahonoora), and out of Heaven High (by High Line), a half-sister to champion Timarida (by Kalaglow). That Irish filly won the Group 1 Irish Champion Stakes, Group 1 Grosser Dallmayr-Preis Bayerisches Zuchtrennen and Grade 1 Beverly D Stakes, and she was third in the Group 1 Champion Stakes. Timarida is the dam of the nine-and-a-half-furlong Group 3 scorer Timarwa (by Daylami), whereas her half-sister Timiya (by High Top) is responsible for the dual Scandinavian champion Heavy Loaded (by Pips Pride), who was effective from six furlongs to a mile.

There is nothing in that distaff line to suggest any particular potential as a stallion – it has been an effective source of racehorses – but Muhaarar stands out as its best representative and also as its quickest. He is by one of the leading members of the Green Desert (by Danzig) sire line, and although some of the early Oasis Dream stallions have got stakes winners without making an impact, they do include rising star Showcasing (sire of Group 1 stars Advertise and Quiet Reflection) and several promising younger horses who are at early stages of their stud careers.

Muhaarar joined the team at Nunnery Stud not long after their hugely influential Green Desert died, and he is one of the most brilliant representatives of that stallion's line. There is an odd misconception among many that sprinter equals early-season juvenile precocity, even though many top sprinters don't hit their best until at least the summer of their three-year-old campaign or, in some cases, as four-year-olds. This horse was a capable two-year-old and can be expected to get some smart summer and autumn juveniles, but his racing and pedigree profiles suggest that his best results will come with his three-year-olds and older horses and that, like his sire, his top performers could come anywhere in the broad five-to-12-furlong range. He has the potential to become the best stallion son of his sire.

SUMMARY DETAILS

Stood in 2016: Nunnery Stud, England
Fee in 2016: £30,000

Career highlights: 7 wins inc July Cup (Gr1), British Champions Sprint Stakes (Gr1), Prix Maurice de Gheest (Gr1), Commonwealth Cup (Gr1), Gimcrack Stakes (Gr2), Greenham Stakes (Gr3), 3rd Middle Park Stakes (Gr1), July Stakes (Gr2), Winkfield Stakes (L)

Standing in 2019: Nunnery Stud, England

Fee in 2019: £30,000

Stallions by his sire include: Captain Gerrard (Gr1), Showcasing (Gr1), Querari (Gr1), Aqlaam (Gr2), Power (Gr2), Approve (Gr3), Arcano (Gr3), Frozen Power (L), Coach House (winners), Gale Force Ten (winners), Morpheus (winners), Reply (winners), Sri Putra (winners), Fountain Of Youth (2yo), Intrinsic (2yo), Muhaarar (2yo), Charming Thought (yearlings), Free Port Lux (yearlings), De Treville (foals)

MUHAARAR (GB) – bay 2012

Oasis Dream (GB)	Green Desert (USA)	Danzig (USA)
		Foreign Courier (USA)
	Hope (IRE)	Dancing Brave (USA)
		Bahamian
Tahrir (IRE)	Linamix (FR)	Mendez (FR)
		Lunadix (FR)
	Miss Sacha (IRE)	Last Tycoon
		Heaven High

SALES YEARLINGS OF 2018

Sold in Euros

bf - Beach Bunny (by High Chaparral) - Goffs - October - €500,000

bc - Prudenzia (by Dansili) - Arqana - August - €420,000

bc - Weekend Fling (by Forest Wildcat) - Goffs - October - €400,000

bc - African Skies (by Johannesburg) - Arqana - August - €280,000

bf - I'm In Love (by Zafonic) - Arqana - August - €250,000

Paix (IRE)   bf - Pacifique (by Montjeu) - Arqana - August - €250,000

Burkhan (IRE)

bf - Avenue Gabriel (by Champs Elysees) - Arqana - August - €190,000 (p/s)
bc - Royal Highness (by Monsun) - Arqana - August - €160,000
bf - Waldjagd (by Observatory) - Arqana - October - €125,000 (p/s)
bf - Mathuna (by Tagula) - Goffs - October - €85,000
bf - Sun Bittern (by Seeking The Gold) - Goffs - October - €85,000
bc - Alasha (by Barathea) - Goffs - October - €80,000
bc - Heroine Chic (by Big Bad Bob) - Goffs - October - €55,000
bf - Queen Of Tara (by Sadler's Wells) - Goffs - October - €45,000
bf - Soudanaise (by Peintre Celebre) - Arqana - October - €30,000
bf - Nepali Princess (by Mr Greeley) - Arqana - October - €25,000
bf - Queen Of Tara (by Sadler's Wells) - Goffs - February - €9,000

Sold in Guineas

Manaajim (IRE)

bf - Queenofthefairies (by Pivotal) - Tattersalls - October - 925,000gns

Khaalis (IRE)

bc - Alexander Goldrun (by Gold Away) - Tattersalls - October - 500,000gns

Mount Marcy (IRE)

bc - Anna's Rock (by Rock Of Gibraltar) - Tattersalls - October - 500,000gns

Unforgetable (IRE)

bf - Annabelle Ja (by Singspiel) - Tattersalls - October - 425,000gns

Winter Thorn (IRE)

bc - Rose Of Summer (by El Prado) - Tattersalls - October - 375,000gns

Peronista (IRE)

bf - Evita (by Selkirk) - Tattersalls - October - 370,000gns

Al Tarmaah (IRE)	bc - How's She Cuttin' (by Shinko Forest) - Tattersalls - October - 350,000gns
	bc - Vanishing Grey (by Verglas) - Tattersalls - October - 350,000gns
Rocky Dreams (GB)	bc - Mrs Greeley (by Mr Greeley) - Tattersalls - October - 300,000gns
Alexej (GB)	bc - Aquatinta (by Samum) - Tattersalls - October - 200,000gns
Yorkshire Gold (GB)	bc - Swift Campaign (by Intikhab) - Tattersalls - October - 160,000gns
Red For All (GB)	bc - All For Laura (by Cadeaux Genereux) - Tattersalls - October - 140,000gns
	bc - Lauren Louise (by Tagula) - Tattersalls - October - 140,000gns
	bf - Lidanski (by Soviet Star) - Tattersalls - October - 130,000gns
	bf - Rose Blossom (by Pastoral Pursuits) - Tattersalls - October - 130,000gns
Eternal Secret (GB)	bf - Walk On Bye (by Danehill Dancer) - Tattersalls - October - 125,000gns
Born To Glory (GB)	bc - Dulcet (by Halling) - Tattersalls - October - 110,000gns
Keep It Brief (GB)	bc - Brevity (by Street Cry) - Tattersalls - October - 100,000gns
Gifted Ruler (GB)	bc - Dubai Bounty (by Dubai Destination) - Tattersalls - October - 100,000gns
	bf - Propel (by Dubawi) - Tattersalls - October - 100,000gns
	bf - Najam (by Singspiel) - Tattersalls - October - 95,000gns
New Number (GB)	bf - Ballymore Celebre (by Peintre Celebre) - Tattersalls - October - 92,000gns
	bf - Demerger (by Distant View) - Tattersalls - October - 90,000gns
	bf - Solola (by Black Sam Bellamy) - Tattersalls - October - 90,000gns

Aim For The Stars (GB)	bf - Long Face (by Whywhywhy) - Tattersalls - October - 85,000gns
	bc - Persario (by Bishop Of Cashel) - Tattersalls - October - 80,000gns (p/s)
	bf - Lonely Ahead (by Rahy) - Tattersalls - October - 78,000gns
	bf - Bright Approach (by New Approach) - Tattersalls - October - 72,000gns
	bf - Al Fareej (by Iffraaj) - Tattersalls - October - 70,000gns
	bc - Riskit Fora Biskit (by Kodiac) - Tattersalls - October - 70,000gns
	bf - Up In Time (by Noverre) - Tattersalls - October - 70,000gns
	bc - Loulwa (by Montjeu) - Tattersalls - October - 65,000gns
	bf - Jellwa (by Iffraaj) - Tattersalls - October - 38,000gns
	bc - Reroute (by Acclamation) - Tattersalls - October - 32,000gns
Katie Bo Kat (GB)	bc - Tropical Paradise (by Verglas) - Tattersalls - November - 32,000gns
	bf - Infamous Angel (by Exceed And Excel) - Tattersalls - November - 20,000gns
	bf - Saadiah (by Dubai Destination) - Tattersalls - October - 11,000gns

Sold in Pounds

bc - Lady Francesca (by Montjeu) - Goffs UK - August - £120,000
bc - Passion Overflow (by Hennessy) - Goffs UK - August - £80,000
bc - New Providence (by Bahamian Bounty) - Goffs UK - August - £16,000

Not Sold (inc. vendor buy-backs)

Baileys Freedom (GB)	bc - Baileys Jubilee (by Bahamian Bounty) - Tattersalls - October

	bf - Ighraa (by Tamayuz) - Tattersalls - October
Katie Bo Kat (GB)	bf - Infamous Angel (by Exceed And Excel) - Goffs UK - August
	bc - Mensoora (by Jet Master) - Tattersalls - October
	bf - Muntyatee (by Dylan Thomas) - Tattersalls - October
	bc - Rainbow Desert (by Dynaformer) - Tattersalls - October
	bc - Shumoos (by Distorted Humor) - Tattersalls - October
	bf - Station House (by Galileo) - Tattersalls - October
	bc - Xceedingly Xcited (by Exceed And Excel) - Tattersalls - October
	bf - Zacheta (by Polish Precedent) - Tattersalls - October

163

FRESHMAN SIRES OF 2019

MUSIC MASTER (GB)

Fourth in a Salisbury maiden on his only start at two, Music Master (by Piccolo) was a stakes-placed winner over seven furlongs at three and runner-up in the six-furlong Group 3 Bengough Stakes at Ascot on his final start of that campaign. He was also pattern-placed as a five-year-old, but at his peak at four when he beat Heeraat and Es Que Love in the Group 3 Hackwood Stakes and finished third to G Force in the Group 1 Sprint Cup at Haydock, earning a Timeform rating of 122.

He is a son of the Group 1 Nunthorpe Stakes winner Piccolo (by Warning), who spent many years at Throckmorton Court Stud – where Music Master began his stallion career – and he is one of three stakes winners out of the multiple scorer Twilight Mistress (by Bin Ajwaad). His half-sister Spring Fling (by Assertive) won a listed sprint, but his half-brother Twilight Son (by Kyllachy) took both the Group 1 Diamond Jubilee Stakes and Group 1 Sprint Cup, was runner-up in the Group 1 British Champions Sprint, and is now a popular member of the team at Cheveley Park Stud, with a large first crop of foals on the ground in 2018, including one that made €95,000 at Goffs in November.

The second and third generations of the pedigree are light, but that winning third dam, Penny Candle (by Be My Guest), was a half-sister to Group 3 Queen Mary Stakes scorer On Tiptoes (by Shareef Dancer), a filly whose blacktype descendants include the speedy pattern winners Violette (by Observatory) and Silca's Gift (by Cadeaux Genereux).

Most of the horses close-up in his pedigree won as three-year-olds and older horses – as he did – so it seems likely that the dams of his offspring will be influential in how they fare as juveniles. He had 14 foals in his first crop, so has small numbers with which to compete against his rivals, but it would be no surprise to see one or two smart ones among them.

SUMMARY DETAILS

Stood in 2016: Throckmorton Court Stud, England
Fee in 2016: £4,000
Career highlights: 3 wins inc Hackwood Stakes (Gr3), 2nd Bengough Stakes (Gr3), King Charles II Stakes (L), 3rd Sprint Cup (Gr1), Abernant Stakes (Gr3), Prix de Cercle (L)

Stallions by his sire include: Hunting Lion (Gr2), Bratimir Hun (winners), Winker Watson (winners), Music Master (2yo)

MUSIC MASTER (GB) – bay 2010

Piccolo (GB)	Warning	Known Fact (USA)
		Slightly Dangerous (USA)
	Woodwind (FR)	Whistling Wind
		Garden Green
Twilight Mistress (GB)	Bin Ajwaad (IRE)	Rainbow Quest (USA)
		Salidar
	By Candlelight (IRE)	Roi Danzig (USA)
		Penny Candle

SALES YEARLINGS OF 2018
Sold in Pounds

Anna Fallow (GB) bf - Beyond The Rainbow (by Mind Games) - Goffs UK - December - £800
bf - Dimashq (by Mtoto) - Goffs UK - December - £800

Not Sold

bg - Front Page News (by Assertive) - Goffs UK - October

MUSTAJEEB (GB)

Two of the things that we look for when assessing the future potential of any young stallion are the strength of his sire line and the presence or absence of any successful stallions in the distaff side of his family. Mustajeeb passes both tests and yet has been somewhat unpopular so far. He began his career at Overbury Stud in Gloucestershire, but covered just 34 mares in his first season, resulting in 20 foals, and he is to stand the 2019 season from a new base, Haras de Fleury in France.

This Timeform 121-rated horse is by the sire of classic sire Tamayuz (by Nayef), is closely related to that horse, represents a branch of the Mr Prospector (by Raise a Native) line, and comes from a branch of the famous sire-producing family of Galileo (by Sadler's Wells), Sea The Stars (by Cape Cross), King's Best (by Kingmambo), and Adlerflug (by In The Wings).

He chased home War Command in the Group 2 Futurity Stakes at the Curragh on the last of three starts at two – earning a Timeform rating of 110 – and kicked off his three-year-old campaign with defeat of Brendan Bracken in the one-mile Group 3 Amethyst Stakes at Leopardstown before taking third to Kingman in the Group 1 Irish 2000 Guineas. The ground was heavy that day but described as good when he landed the Group 3 Jersey Stakes at Royal Ascot a few weeks later. He then chased home half-length winner Bow Creek in the Group 2 Boomerang Stakes over a mile at Leopardstown, was beaten by less than five lengths when out of the frame behind Karakontie in the Grade 1 Breeders' Cup Mile at Santa Anita, and made a winning return at four to beat Maarek in the Group 2 Greenlands Stakes over six at the Curragh. His final start was a somewhat disappointing fifth to Undrafted in the Group 1 Diamond Jubilee Stakes at Ascot a month later, and his Timeform mark that season was 119.

Mustajeeb is the best of several foals out of Rifqah (by Elusive Quality), and that half-sister to ill-fated Group 3 Prix Miesque winner Aboulie (by Exceed And Excel) is a daughter of Anja (by Indian Ridge), a half-sister to classic star and somewhat successful sire Anabaa Blue (by Anabaa). Anja's siblings also include the stakes-winning fillies Measured Tempo (by Sadler's Wells) and Reunite (by Kingmambo) and the notably successful broodmare Al Ishq (by Nureyev). That one's blacktype offspring are headed

167

by the aforementioned Group 1-winning miler and classic sire Tamayuz.

Third dam Allez Les Trois (by Riverman) won the Group 3 Prix de Flore over 10 and a half furlongs at Saint-Cloud, and as she is out of Allegretta (by Lombard) she is, of course, a half-sister to Group 1 Prix de l'Arc de Triomphe heroine and phenomenal broodmare Urban Sea (by Miswaki). The dam of Derby heroes and outstanding stallions Galileo and Sea The Stars, plus the top-level winners Black Sam Bellamy (by Sadler's Wells) and My Typhoon (by Giant's Causeway), her many descendants of note include Group/Grade 1 stars Bracelet (by Montjeu), Athena (by Camelot) and Masar (by New Approach). Urban Sea's siblings include classic star and classic sire King's Best, her three-parts brother Tertullian (by Miswaki) was a leading sire in Germany, and if you go back another generation and look at the descendants of Allegretta's siblings then you will find top-level winners such as A Raving Beauty (by Mastercraftsman), Azzurro (by Bluebird), and the aforementioned Adlerflug.

Mustajeeb was a classic-placed, Group 2-winning sprinter-miler whom Timeform rated 121, he represents one of the most famous stallion-producing families in the world, and every blacktype success for his close relation Tamayuz is another advert for his potential. What a pity then that he faces such an uphill battle. Some of his offspring will win as two-year-olds, but his best results look likely to come from three-year-olds and older horses, likely in the broad six-to-12-furlong range.

SUMMARY DETAILS

Stood in 2016: Overbury Stud, England
Fee in 2016: £5,000
Career highlights: 4 wins inc Greenlands Stakes (Gr2), Jersey Stakes (Gr3), Amethyst Stakes (Gr3), 2nd Boomerang Mile (Gr2), Futurity Stakes (Gr2), 3rd Irish 2000 Guineas (Gr1)
Standing in 2019: Haras de Fleury, France
Fee in 2019: €2,000
Stallions by his sire include: Tamayuz (Gr1), Valirann (3yo), Mustajeeb (2yo)

MUSTAJEEB (GB) – chestnut 2011

Nayef (USA)	Gulch (USA)	Mr Prospector (USA)
		Jameela (USA)
	Height Of Fashion (FR)	Bustino
		Highclere
Rifqah (USA)	Elusive Quality (USA)	Gone West (USA)
		Touch Of Greatness (USA)
	Anja (IRE)	Indian Ridge
		Allez Les Trois (USA)

SALES YEARLINGS OF 2018

Sold in Euros

bf - Kafaala (by Shamardal) - Goffs - November - €20,000
bf - Unequivocal (by Observatory) - Arqana - November - €6,000
bc - Albida (by Dansili) - Arqana - October - €4,000
bf - Lukrecia (by Exceed And Excel) - Arqana - November - €4,000
chc - Dance Away (by Pivotal) - Goffs - November - €2,000 (p/s)
chc - Trump Street (by First Trump) - Tatts IRE - September - €2,000
bc - Ghaidaa (by Cape Cross) - Goresbridge - October - €1,600
chf - Felwah (by Aqlaam) - Goresbridge - October - €1,100

Sold in Guineas

bc - Shemriyna (by King Of Kings) - Tattersalls - October - 28,000gns

Sold in Pounds

Intimate Moment (GB)   bf - Firebelly (by Nicolotte) - Tatts IRE Ascot - September - £10,500

Not Sold (inc. vendor buy-backs)

chc - Dance Away (by Pivotal) - Goffs - February

bf - Mahsooba (by Hard Spun) - Goffs -
November
bc - Shemriyna (by King Of Kings) -
Tattersalls - November
chc - Transvaal Sky (by Avonbridge) -
Goffs UK - October

NIGHT OF THUNDER (IRE)

Winner of a late-season Goodwood maiden and a listed contest at Doncaster – both over six furlongs – by a combined margin of nine lengths, Night Of Thunder (by Dubawi) lost his unbeaten record when chasing home Kingman in the Group 3 Greenham Stakes first time out at three but gained some revenge for that defeat when taking what turned out to be one of the best editions of the Group 1 2000 Guineas in recent decades. He beat Kingman by half a length, Australia was a head back in third, Shifting Power was fourth, and Charm Spirit fifth, with Kingston Hill another length and a half away in eighth, a length in front of 10th-placed The Grey Gatsby.

Australia, Kingston Hill and The Grey Gatsby earned their fame when stepping up in trip, and both Kingman and Charm Spirit went on to become multiple mile Group 1 stars, so it was remarkable that Night Of Thunder managed to win just once more in his career, when beating Toormore by a neck in the Group 1 Lockinge Stakes 12 months later. Timeform rated him 110p at two, 127 at three, and 123 at four, and he was understandably popular in his first season at Kildangan Stud, covering 137 mares. A low double-digit tally of his initial yearlings made six-figure sums at auction, he moved to Dalham Hall Stud in 2018 and is there again this year.

The early Dubawi (by Dubai Millennium) stallions include Makfi and Poet's Voice – both of whom have sired Group 1 winners (Makfi has four, Poet's Voice two) – but most of his best sons are in earlier stages of their stud careers or are still in training, so it's still too early to know what sort of profile he will develop as a sire of stallions.

Night Of Thunder is out of the stakes-placed Forest Storm (by Galileo), and that half-sister to Indian classic scorer New Appliance (by Burden Of Proof) is out of Quiet Storm (by Desert Prince), a stakes-placed granddaughter of Group 1 Irish 1000 Guineas heroine Forest Flower (by Green Forest). A first-crop representative of her sire and out of Group 1 Oaks third Leap Lively (by Nijinsky), she was also the top-rated juvenile filly in England in a season where she had a great rivalry with Minstrella. Forest Flower won the Group 3 Queen Mary Stakes, Group 3 Cherry Hinton Stakes and Group 2 Mill Reef Stakes but was runner-up to Minstrella in the Group 1 Phoenix Stakes. That rival then added the Group 1 Moyglare Stud Stakes, but when the pair met again in the Group 1 Cheveley Park Stakes, it was the petite Forest Flower who hit the line first. Sadly, she lost the race in the stewards' room, so the grey became a triple top-level winner.

Being a Dubawi out of a direct descendant of Forest Flower gave Night Of Thunder every chance of being a top-class racehorse, but it leaves him as something of an unknown as a stallion prospect, although his early support and auction success augur well for his future. His two-year-old winners are likely to be seen to better effect in the latter half of the season, his best offspring are likely to be competitive in the broad six-to-12-furlong range, and there is every reason to hope that he can do as well in this second career as he did on the track.

SUMMARY DETAILS

Stood in 2016: Kildangan Stud, Ireland
Fee in 2016: €30,000
Career highlights: 4 wins inc 2000 Guineas (Gr1), Lockinge Stakes (Gr1), Doncaster Stakes (Listed), 2nd Queen Elizabeth II Stakes (Gr1), St James's Palace Stakes (Gr1), Greenham Stakes (Gr3), 3rd Prix du Moulin de Longchamp (Gr1)
Standing in 2019: Dalham Hall Stud, England
Fee in 2019: £15,000
Stallions by his sire include: Makfi (Gr1), Poet's Voice (Gr1), Al Kazeem (L), Akeed Mofeed (winners), Monterosso (winners), Universal (winners), Waldpark (winners), Wilful Default (winners), Worthadd (winners), Hunter's Light (2yo), Night Of Thunder (2yo), Red Dubawi (2yo), Willow Magic (2yo), New Bay (yearlings), Dartmouth (foals), Erupt (foals), Postponed (foals), Time Test (foals), Zarak (foals)

NIGHT OF THUNDER (IRE) – chestnut 2011

Dubawi (IRE)	Dubai Millennium (GB)	Seeking The Gold (USA)
		Colorado Dancer
	Zomaradah (GB)	Deploy
		Jawaher (IRE)
Forest Storm (GB)	Galileo (IRE)	Sadler's Wells (USA)
		Urban Sea (USA)
	Quiet Storm (IRE)	Desert Prince (IRE)
		Hertford Castle (GB)

SALES YEARLINGS OF 2018

Sold in Euros

Man Of The Night (FR) bc - Mandheera (by Bernardini) - Arqana - August - €350,000

Moving Light (IRE) chc - North East Bay (by Prospect Bay) - Tatts IRE - September - €180,000

Opening Night (IRE) chf - Varsity (by Lomitas) - Arqana - August - €130,000

Lady Lilnoi (GB) bf - True Match (by Cape Cross) - Arqana - August - €110,000

bc - Shama's Song (by Teofilo) - Goffs - October - €105,000

chc - Permission Slip (by Authorized) - Goffs - October - €65,000

bc - Blameless (by Authorized) - Goffs - October - €60,000

Wonderwork (IRE) bc - First Party (by Royal Applause) - Tatts IRE - September - €52,000

chc - Que Sera Sera (by Dansili) - Goffs - October - €52,000

bc - Mujabaha (by Redoute's Choice) - Arqana - October - €42,000

bf - Love And Laughter (by Theatrical) - Tatts IRE - September - €26,000

chf - Giveupyeraulsins (by Mark Of Esteem) - Tatts IRE - September - €23,000

chf - Refusetolisten (by Clodovil) - Tatts IRE - September - €22,000

bf - Royal Guinevere (by Invincible Spirit) - Tatts IRE - September - €22,000

bf - Thames Pageant (by Dansili) - Goffs - October - €17,000

Keeping My Baby (FR) chf - Keeping Quiet (by Samum) - Arqana - October - €15,000

bc - Suggest (by Raven's Pass) - Tatts IRE - September - €10,000

chc - Tornadea (by Sea The Stars) - Arqana - November - €7,500

grf - Corrine (by Spectrum) - Goffs -
October - €5,000

Sold in Guineas

| | |
chc - Aris (by Danroad) - Tattersalls -
October - 260,000gns
Khurshed (IRE)   chc - Award (by Tamayuz) - Tattersalls -
October - 200,000gns
chc - Cantal (by Pivotal) - Tattersalls -
October - 160,000gns
Owhatanight (GB)   grc - White Wedding (by Green Desert)
- Tattersalls - October - 155,000gns
chc - Ermine And Velvet (by Nayef) -
Tattersalls - October - 115,000gns
Sun Power (FR)   bc - Sparkling Smile (by Cape Cross) -
Tattersalls - October - 115,000gns
Desert Destination (IRE) bc - Scarlett Rose (by Royal Applause) -
Tattersalls - October - 90,000gns
Godfather (IRE)   chc - Aqlaam Vision (by Aqlaam) -
Tattersalls - October - 80,000gns
bc - Souviens Toi (by Dalakhani) -
Tattersalls - October - 70,000gns
chc - Emreliya (by Danehill Dancer) -
Tattersalls - October - 62,000gns
Dalanijujo (IRE)   chf - Kiss From A Rose (by Compton
Place) - Tattersalls - October -
60,000gns
chf - Broadway Duchess (by New
Approach) - Tattersalls - October -
50,000gns (p/s)
chf - Fair Hill (by New Approach) -
Tattersalls - October - 50,000gns
chf - Time Over (by Mark Of Esteem) -
Tattersalls - October - 50,000gns
chc - Sunset Avenue (by Street Cry) -
Tattersalls - October - 48,000gns
bc - Raskutani (by Dansili) - Tattersalls -
October - 38,000gns
chf - Silent Serenade (by Bertolini) -
Tattersalls - October - 37,000gns

Atmospheric (GB)
bf - Havergate (by Dansili) - Tattersalls - October - 36,000gns
bf - Look Busy (by Danetime) - Tattersalls - October - 34,000gns
bc - Alaia (by Sinndar) - Tattersalls - October - 22,000gns
bf - Mathanora (by Anabaa) - Tattersalls - October - 20,000gns
bc - Pencarrow (by Green Desert) - Tattersalls - October - 20,000gns
bc - Palimony (by Oasis Dream) - Tattersalls - October - 13,000gns
chf - Areyaam (by Elusive Quality) - Tattersalls - October - 11,000gns
bc - Powdermill (by Oasis Dream) - Tattersalls - October - 10,000gns
bc - Darrfonah (by Singspiel) - Tattersalls - November - 8,000gns
chf - Neshla (by Singspiel) - Tattersalls - October - 8,000gns (p/s)
bc - Rezyana (by Redoute's Choice) - Tattersalls - October - 8,000gns
bf - Jumeirah Palm Star (by Invincible Spirit) - Tattersalls - October - 6,000gns
bc - Sultanah Heyam (by Manduro) - Tattersalls - October - 4,000gns

Sold in Pounds
Perfected (GB)
chc - Semayyel (by Green Desert) - Goffs UK - August - £74,000
chf - Aljaazya (by Speightstown) - Goffs UK - August - £60,000
chf - Doregan (by Bahhare) - Goffs UK - August - £40,000
chf - Elegant Peace (by Intense Focus) - Goffs UK - August - £40,000 (p/s)
bf - Many Colours (by Green Desert) - Goffs UK - August - £38,000
chf - Step Sequence (by Nayef) - Goffs UK - August - £32,000

chc - Yukon Girl (by Manduro) - Goffs
UK - August - £2,000 (p/s)

Not Sold (inc. vendor buy-backs)

	bc - Al Nassa (by Bernardini) - Tatts IRE - September
	bc - Amallna (by Green Desert) - Tattersalls - October
	bf - Cape Castle (by Cape Cross) - Tatts IRE - September
	bf - Cape Good Hope (by Cape Cross) - Tattersalls - October
	chf - Dinvar Diva (by Dalakhani) - Tattersalls - October
	chc - Doors To Manual (by Royal Academy) - Tattersalls - October
Herr Juergensen (IRE)	bc - Leala (by Montjeu) - Goffs - February
Herr Juergensen (IRE)	bc - Leala (by Montjeu) - Baden-Baden - May
	bc - Marmoom Flower (by Cape Cross) - Arqana - August
	bc - Midwifery (by Teofilo) - Goffs - October
	bf - Mill Guineas (by Salse) - Goffs UK - August
	bf - Mystic Melody (by Montjeu) - Arqana - August
No Limit Credit (GER)	bf - Nasrine (by Barathea) - Baden-Baden - August
	bf - Pure Illusion (by Danehill) - Tattersalls - November
	bc - Regal Hawk (by Singspiel) - Tattersalls - October
	bf - Storyland (by Menifee) - Tattersalls - October

NIGHT OF THUNDER (IRE)

NUTAN (IRE)

A classic-winning son of the now South Africa-based, regally related multiple Group 1 star Duke Of Marmalade (by Danehill), Nutan took the Group 1 Deutsches Derby by five lengths on good ground, he stands in Germany and seems unlikely to have many runners outside of that country over the next couple of years.

He is a half-brother to middle-distance Group 1 heroine Nymphea (by Dylan Thomas) and also to Navaro Girl (by Holy Roman Emperor), the 10-furlong Group 3 scorer who finished third to Nonza in the Group 1 Darley Prix Jean Romanet at Deauville last summer. His dam, Neele (by Peintre Celebre), was a head runner-up in an 11-furlong Group 3 on soft ground at Hamburg, and her siblings feature Group 2 Oaks d'Italia winner Night Of Magic (by Peintre Celebre), the dam of classic-placed dual Group 1 Preis von Europa heroine Nightflower (by Dylan Thomas).

Grandam Night Teeny (by Platini) also has a star sibling as she is a half-sister to Night Petticoat (by Petoski), the Group 2 Preis der Diana (German Oaks)-winning dam of Group 1 Deutsches Derby hero Next Desert (by Desert Style) and Group 1 Preis der Diana winner Next Gina (by Perugino). The latter died young, but her dual stakes-winning daughter Nina Celebre (by Peintre Celebre) is the dam of Hong Kong Group 1 star and multi-millionaire Pakistan Star (by Shamardal).

All of this makes Gestut Lindenhof stallion Nutan an interesting prospect, and it would be no surprise to see him get some good results in Germany.

SUMMARY DETAILS

Stood in 2016: Gestut Lindenhof, Germany
Fee in 2016: €3,500
Career highlights: 2 wins inc Deutsches Derby (Gr1), 3rd
Grosser Preis von Berlin (Gr1), Oppenheim-Union-Rennen (Gr2)
Standing in 2019: Gestut Erftmuhle, Germany
Fee in 2019: €3,000
Stallions by his sire include: Nutan (2yo), Moofeed (yearlings)

NUTAN (IRE) – bay 2012

Duke Of Marmalade (IRE)	Danehill (USA)	Danzig (USA)
		Razyana (USA)
	Love Me True (USA)	Kingmambo (USA)
		Lassie's Lady (USA)
Neele (IRE)	Peintre Celebre (USA)	Nureyev (USA)
		Peinture Bleue (USA)
	Night Teeny (GB)	Platini (GER)
		Nightrockette

SALES YEARLINGS OF 2018

Sold in Euros

bc - Fareia (by Areion) - BBAG - October - €10,000
brc - Numero Uno (by Lavirco) - BBAG - October - €9,000
brf - Schante (by Dai Jin) - BBAG - October - €2,500
brf - Lady In Red (by General Assembly) - BBAG - October - €1,500

Not Sold

bc - Fareia (by Areion) - Baden-Baden - August
bf - Lady Di (by Samum) - BBAG - October
chf - Quezon (by Liquido) - BBAG - October
chf - Warrior Czarina (by Pleasantly Perfect) - BBAG - October

OUTSTRIP (GB)

Timeform-rated 116 at two and three years of age, Outstrip (by Exceed And Excel) was a popular addition to the team at Dalham Hall Stud and there were 86 foals from his initial triple-digit book. He won the Grade 1 Breeders' Cup Juvenile Turf and the Group 2 Champagne Stakes, finished third to Kingman in the Group 1 St James's Palace Stakes, and looks likely to get his best winners at up to 10 furlongs, with some potentially getting a bit farther. His two-year-olds are likely to be seen to best effect in the autumn.

The best representative of nine-furlong Grade 1 winner Asi Siempre (by El Prado), he is a great-grandson of the Group 3 Cherry Hinton Stakes and Group 3 Park Stakes winner Turkish Treasure (by Sir Ivor), which means that his unraced grandam, Siempre Asi (by Silver Hawk), is a half-sister to Group 3 Norfolk Stakes winner Magic Mirror (by Nureyev). That colt, who was also fourth in the Group 1 Phoenix Stakes, sired some winners from limited opportunities, his siblings included pattern-placed juvenile listed winner Treasure Trove (by Try My Best) and also Exciting (by Mill Reef), the mare who gave us Almushtarak (by Fairy King) and Tiber (by Titus Livius). The latter excelled in Hong Kong, whereas Group 2-winning miler Almushtarak was placed in the Group 1 Queen Elizabeth II Stakes, Group 1 Lockinge Stakes and two editions of the Group 1 Sussex Stakes, hitting a peak end-of-season Timeform rating of 122.

Outstrip's initial yearlings found favour in the middle to lower end of the market, he is by the sire of the somewhat successful young sires Excelebration, Helmet, and current freshman Sidestep – each of whom has a Group 1 star to his name – and it will be interesting to see how his second career turns out.

SUMMARY DETAILS

Stood in 2016: Dalham Hall Stud, England
Fee in 2016: £5,000
Career highlights: 3 wins inc Breeders' Cup Juvenile Turf (Gr1), Champagne Stakes (Gr2), 2nd Vintage Stakes (Gr2), 3rd St James's Palace Stakes (Gr1), Dewhurst Stakes (Gr1)
Standing in 2019: Dalham Hall Stud, England
Fee in 2019: £5,000

Stallions by his sire include: Excelebration (Gr1), Helmet (Gr1), Sidestep (Gr1), Bungle Inthejungle (Gr3), Exceedingly Good (Gr3), Burwaaz (winners), Kuroshio (winners), Fulbright (2yo), Outstrip (2yo), Buratino (yearlings), Cotai Glory (foals), James Garfield (new)

OUTSTRIP (GB) – grey 2011

Exceed And Excel (AUS)	Danehill (USA)	Danzig (USA)
		Razyana (USA)
	Patrona (USA)	Lomond (USA)
		Gladiolus (USA)
Asi Siempre (USA)	El Prado (IRE)	Sadler's Wells (USA)
		Lady Capulet (USA)
	Siempre Asi (USA)	Silver Hawk (USA)
		Turkish Treasure (USA)

SALES YEARLINGS OF 2018

Sold in Euros

	grc - Mrs Micawber (by Nayef) - Arqana - August - €62,000
	bc - Sarvana (by Dubai Destination) - Arqana - August - €60,000
	bc - Abandagold (by Orpen) - Arqana - October - €40,000
La La Land (GER)	chf - La Caldera (by Hernando) - BBAG - October - €38,000
Speed Dating (FR)	bc - Sign Your Name (by Areion) - Arqana - October - €37,000
	grc - Ella Fitz (by Pivotal) - Arqana - August - €35,000
	bf - Singing Field (by Singspiel) - Tatts IRE - September - €35,000
	bf - Lune Orientale (by Dalakhani) - Arqana - October - €33,000
	bc - Demeanour (by Giant's Causeway) - Arqana - October - €30,000 (p/s)
	bf - Daidoo (by Shamardal) - Arqana - August - €25,000
	bc - Polly Adler (by Fantastic Light) - Tatts IRE - September - €23,000

bc - Bocca Bianca (by Saddex) - Osarus - September - €18,000 (p/s)

bf - Medalha Milagrosa (by Miner's Mark) - Osarus - September - €17,000

bf - Angel Oak (by Teofilo) - Arqana - October - €16,000

brc - Daring Damsel (by Van Nistelrooy) - Tatts IRE - September - €14,000 (p/s)

bc - Wings Of Fame (by Namid) - Tatts IRE - September - €14,000

bf - Danse Revee (by Manduro) - Arqana - October - €13,000

grc - Speak Softly To Me (by Ogygian) - Tatts IRE - September - €13,000

bc - Zarara (by Manila) - Goffs - October - €12,000

bc - Church Melody (by Oasis Dream) - Tatts IRE - September - €10,000

Kings Turf (GER)   bc - Konigin Shuttle (by Big Shuffle) - BBAG - October - €10,000

grc - Winterbourne (by Cadeaux Genereux) - Tatts IRE - September - €10,000

grf - Rangooned (by Bahamian Bounty) - Goffs - November - €7,000

chc - Tazyeen (by Tamayuz) - Goffs - October - €6,000

chc - Tazyaan (by Tamayuz) - BBAG - October - €6,000

bc - Visual Element (by Distant View) - Arqana - October - €5,000

grf - Floating (by Oasis Dream) - Goffs - February - €4,000

Place Pereire (FR)   bf - Fusca (by Lando) - Arqana - November - €4,000

grc - Honeymead (by Pivotal) - Tatts IRE - September - €4,000

bc - Candy Banter (by Distorted Humor) - Goffs - October - €3,000

brf - Assumption (by Beckett) - Goffs -
November - €2,800
bf - Chicane (by Motivator) - Goffs -
November - €1,000

Sold in Guineas

chc - Pink Flames (by Redback) -
Tattersalls - October - 50,000gns
chc - Snake's Head (by Golden Snake) -
Tattersalls - October - 30,000gns
chc - Tawjeeh (by Haafhd) - Tattersalls -
October - 27,000gns
bf - Sahool (by Unfuwain) - Tattersalls -
October - 25,000gns
b/grf - Makara (by Lion Cavern) -
Tattersalls - October - 23,000gns
chc - Quinine (by Dark Angel) -
Tattersalls - November - 15,000gns
grc - Ariyfa (by Cape Cross) - Tattersalls
- October - 7,000gns
bf - Foundation Filly (by Lando) -
Tattersalls - October - 3,500gns
grf - Fenella Rose (by Compton Place) -
Tattersalls - October - 3,000gns
bf - Lady Benedicte (by Shamardal) -
Tattersalls - October - 3,000gns
chc - Sakhiza (by Sakhee) - Tattersalls -
October - 1,500gns
chf - Roxy Hart (by Halling) - Tattersalls
- October - 800gns

Sold in Pounds

Agent Zero (FR)　　　　grc - Miss Vendome (by Medicean) -
Goffs UK - August - £65,000
Laughing Crusader (GB) blc - Sitting Pritty (by Compton Place) -
Goffs UK - August - £42,000
Bermuda Schwartz (GB) grc - Almaviva (by Grand Lodge) -
Goffs UK - August - £38,000
brc - Cosmea (by Compton Place) -
Goffs UK - August - £28,000

chc - Perfect Muse (by Oasis Dream) -
Goffs UK - August - £28,000
bc - Cheerfully (by Sadler's Wells) -
Goffs UK - August - £15,000
bc - Mudammera (by Dubawi) - Tatts
IRE Ascot - September - £12,000
grf - Rancho Montoya (by High
Chaparral) - Goffs UK - August -
£11,000
grc - Shaken And Stirred (by Cadeaux
Genereux) - Goffs UK - August -
£11,000

Beat The Breeze (GB)   grc - Tranquil Flight (by Oasis Dream) -
Tatts IRE Ascot - September - £11,000
grf - A Mind Of Her Own (by Danehill
Dancer) - Goffs UK - August - £10,000
grf - Celsius Degre (by Verglas) - Tatts
IRE Ascot - September - £10,000
grf - Strasbourg Place (by Compton
Place) - Goffs UK - August - £9,500
grc - Silent Waters (by Polish Precedent)
- Goffs UK - October - £7,500
chc - Laurena (by Acatenango) - Goffs
UK - October - £7,000 (p/s)
bc - Fidelio's Miracle (by Mountain Cat)
- Tatts IRE Ascot - September - £2,500
chf - Don't Tell Bertie (by Bertolini) -
Goffs UK - October - £2,000
chf - Starving Faithful (by Makfi) -
Goffs UK - October - £800 (p/s)

Not Sold (inc. vendor buy-backs)

bf - Aswaaq (by Peintre Celebre) -
Goffs UK - October
bc - Black Sheba (by Aqlaam) - Tatts
IRE Ascot - November
grf - Brazilian Flame (by Camacho) -
Tatts IRE - September
chf - Dularame (by Pivotal) - Tattersalls
- October

OUTSTRIP (GB)

	bg - Fiducia (by Lawman) - Tatts IRE Ascot - August
	grf - Floating (by Oasis Dream) - Tatts IRE Ascot - September
	chc - Gandini (by Night Shift) - Tatts IRE - September
	blc - Gennie Bond (by Pivotal) - Tatts IRE Ascot - November
	blg - Hilden (by Dansili) - Goffs UK - October
	chc - Lady Atlas (by Dutch Art) - Tatts IRE - September
Smokey (GB)	grf - Lady Tabitha (by Tamayuz) - Tattersalls - October
	chc - Love And War (by War Blade) - Osarus - September
Zero Limits (GB)	grc - Mpumalanga (by Observatory) - Tattersalls - October
	brc - Navajo Chant (by Cape Cross) - Goffs UK - August
	b/brc - Nouvelle Lune (by Fantastic Light) - Tattersalls - October
	bf - Oulianovsk (by Peintre Celebre) - Baden-Baden - August
	grf - Primula (by Dansili) - Goffs - November
	bf - Sunny Side Up (by Refuse To Bend) - Tattersalls - October

185

PETHER'S MOON (IRE)

Group 1 Coronation Cup winner Pether's Moon (by Dylan Thomas) is standing at Yorton Farm Stud in Wales, had 40 foals in his first crop and is attracting attention in the National Hunt sector. The Timeform 121-rated is among the best representatives of his Arc and classic-winning sire and is a grandson of Danehill (by Danzig) whose influence on the global flat racing industry has been phenomenal. This male line has been getting more blacktype winners under National Hunt rules in recent years.

His dam, Softly Tread, won the Group 3 Gladness Stakes and Listed Tyros Stakes, both over seven furlongs, and that daughter of dual Guineas hero Tirol (by Thatching) comes from a family that has produced a variety of blacktype horses without getting any stars.

It remains to be seen if he will have any more than just the occasional runner on the flat, and his long-term potential appears to be as a sire of bumper horses, point-to-pointers, hurdlers, and chasers.

SUMMARY DETAILS

Stood in 2016: Yorton Farm Stud, Wales
Fee in 2016: £2,250
Career highlights: 7 wins inc Coronation Cup (Gr1), International Bosphorus Cup (Gr2), Cumberland Lodge Stakes (Gr3), Glorious Stakes (Gr3), Floodlit Stakes (L), 2nd Jockey Club Stakes (Gr2), John Porter Stakes (Gr3), Buckhounds Stakes (L), 3rd Jockey Club Stakes (Gr2), Hardwicke Stakes (Gr2), Princess of Wales's Stakes (Gr2)
Standing in 2019: Yorton Farm Stud, Wales
Fee in 2019: private
Stallions by his sire include: Pether's Moon (2yo), Dylan Mouth (new)

PETHER'S MOON (IRE) – bay 2010

Dylan Thomas (IRE)	Danehill (USA)	Danzig (USA)
		Razyana (USA)
	Lagrion (USA)	Diesis
		Wrap It Up
Softly Tread (IRE)	Tirol	Thatching
		Alpine Niece
	Second Guess	Ela-Mana-Mou
		Warning Sound

SALES YEARLINGS OF 2018

Sold in Euros

bc - Corbetstown Queen (by Oscar) - Tatts IRE - February - €20,000
bc - Bochafina (by High Chaparral) - Goffs - November - €15,000
bc - Song Of The Desert (by Desert Sun) - Arqana - November - €7,000

Sold in Pounds

brc - Pont Royal (by Trempolino) - Goffs UK - January - £5,000
bf - Sovereignsflagship (by Supreme Leader) - Goffs UK - January - £2,000
bc - Manyshadesofblack (by Tikkanen) - Goffs UK - January - £800

Not Sold

bc - Miss Duffy (by Sir Harry Lewis) - Goffs UK - January

PRINCE GIBRALTAR (FR)

A high-class performer at two, three and four years of age, Haras de Montaigu stallion Prince Gibraltar (by Rock Of Gibraltar) is by the sire of Group 1-siring stallions Mount Nelson and Society Rock, and he had 52 foals in his first crop. Timeform rated him 116 at two, 124 at three and 125 at four, his top-level wins came in the 10-furlong Criterium de Saint-Cloud and 12-furlong Grosser Preis von Baden, and his string of notable placings included third to The Grey Gatsby in the Group 1 Prix du Jockey Club (French Derby).

He is a full-brother to listed scorer Princess Gibraltar, his dam is five-time winner Princess Sofia (by Pennekamp), and that mare's siblings include stakes winner and notable broodmare Queen Catherine (by Machiavellian) – the dam of Group 3 winner and Group 1 Oaks d'Italia runner-up Lady Catherine (by Bering). That filly is, in turn, the grandam of Group 2 Duchess of Cambridge Stakes heroine and Group 1 Cheveley Park Stakes runner-up Illuminate (by Zoffany).

Third dam Princess Karenda (by Gummo) won the Grade 1 Hollywood Oaks and Grade 1 Santa Margarita Invitational Handicap, and that mare's siblings include Big Puddles (by Delta Judge), the Grade 3-winning dam of Grade 1-placed Grade 2 scorer and somewhat successful sire Thunder Puddles (by Speak John).

Two-year-old winners for Prince Gibraltar are likely to come late in the season, and although he may get the occasional miler, he promises to get his best results in the middle-distance and staying divisions.

SUMMARY DETAILS
Stood in 2016: Haras de la Reboursiere et de Montaigu, France
Fee in 2016: €3,000
Career highlights: 4 wins inc Grosser Preis von Baden (Gr1), Criterium de Saint-Cloud (Gr1), Prix Greffulhe (Gr2), 2nd Grand Prix de Paris (Gr1), Grosser Preis von Bayern (Gr1), Grand Prix de Chantilly (Gr2), 3rd Prix du Jockey-Club (Gr1), Prix Guillaume d'Ornano (Gr2), York Stakes (Gr2)
Standing in 2019: Haras de Montaigu, France
Fee in 2019: €3,000

Stallions by his sire include: Mount Nelson (Gr1), Red Rock Canyon (Gr1), Seventh Rock (Gr1), Society Rock (Gr1), Murtajill (L), Proart (L), Golden Archer (winners), High Rock (winners), Varenar (winners), Prince Gibraltar (2yo)

PRINCE GIBRALTAR (FR) – chestnut 2011

Rock Of Gibraltar (IRE)	Danehill (USA)	Danzig (USA)
		Razyana (USA)
	Offshore Boom	Be My Guest (USA)
		Push A Button
Princess Sofia (UAE)	Pennekamp (USA)	Bering
		Coral Dance (FR)
	Russian Royal (USA)	Nureyev (USA)
		Princess Karenda (USA)

SALES YEARLINGS OF 2018

Sold in Euros

Nulparailleurs (FR) — bc - Etrangere (by Fusaichi Pegasus) - Arqana - October - €30,000

Siavash (FR) — bc - Sizal (by Sicyos) - Arqana - October - €28,000
bc - Diamond Star (by Daylami) - Osarus - September - €19,000
chf - Dauphine (by Rich Man's Gold) - Osarus - September - €15,000
bc - Moune (by Whipper) - Osarus - September - €15,000

My Charming Prince (FR) — chc - Hello Sindarella (by Sinndar) - Arqana - October - €14,000

Cote Jardin (FR) — chc - Perspective (by Funambule) - Arqana - November - €13,000

Pont D'Ouilly (FR) — chc - Pragmatisme (by Linngari) - Arqana - October - €11,000
bf - Holiday Maker (by Dubai Destination) - Arqana - October - €10,000
bf - Yours Ever (by Dansili) - Arqana - October - €10,000
bf - Belle Chasse (by Kyllachy) - Arqana - October - €9,000 (p/s)

Fashion Princess (FR)	bf - Fashion School (by Shamardal) - Osarus - September - €9,000 (p/s) chc - Charming Clem (by Mastercraftsman) - Arqana - October - €8,000
Sanak (FR)	bc - Sanadora (by Manduro) - Arqana - November - €8,000
Napadla (FR)	bf - Bainorama (by Anabaa) - Arqana - November - €5,500
Song Princess (FR)	bf - Song Of Hope (by Monsun) - Arqana - November - €3,500
On Canvas (FR)	bf - Famous Portrait (by Kendor) - Arqana - October - €3,000 (p/s) bf - Roxanne (by Falco) - Arqana - October - €3,000 (p/s)
Sanak (FR)	bc - Sanadora (by Manduro) - Arqana - February - €3,000 (p/s) bf - Scarlet Sonnet (by Invincible Spirit) - Arqana - November - €2,000

Not Sold (inc. vendor buy-backs)

	bf - Don't Hurry Me (by Hurricane Run) - Arqana - October
Manhattan Garden (FR)	chg - Manhattan Princess (by Pivotal) - Arqana - November
Charlotte Jag (FR)	chf - Reine Bere (by Until Sundown) - Arqana - November
Gagnante (FR)	bf - Sybilia (by Spectrum) - Arqana - November
Sur Les Roques (FR)	bc - Upper Jem (by Bertolini) - Goffs - December bc - Zongoraora (by Bering) - Arqana - October

FRESHMAN SIRES OF 2019

RED DUBAWI (IRE)

A talented performer from six to 10 furlongs and Group 1 winner in Italy at a mile, Red Dubawi (by Dubawi) is by the sire of successful stallions Makfi and Poet's Voice, he is out of Group 3-placed middle-distance stakes winner Maredsous (by Homme De Loi), and comes from a less distinguished family than do most by his sire.

His grandam, Tutti (by Rahotep), won seven times from two to five years of age and she is also responsible for Fontaine Guerard (by Homme De Loi), a stakes-placed dual winner who has produced pattern-placed stakes winner Fontcia (by Enrique) and the listed hurdles scorer Font Froide (by Trempolino).

Red Dubawi was bred by Haras Des Sablonnets, where he spent his first two seasons, he stood at Haras de la Croix Sonnet in 2018, and there were 41 foals in his first crop, six of whom are AQPS (autre que pur sang). His flat winners are likely to be effective anywhere from a mile to two and a half miles, and it may be that his long-term prospects are as a National Hunt stallion.

SUMMARY DETAILS

Stood in 2016: Haras des Sablonnets, France
Fee in 2016: €2,000
Career highlights: 5 wins inc Premio Vittorio di Capua (Gr1), Grosser Preis der CGH Versicherungen (Gr2), Badener Meile (Gr3), Prix Pelleas (L), 2nd Prix de Boulogne (L), 3rd Meilen Trophy (Gr2), Grosser Preis der Wirtschaft (Gr3), Waterford Testimonal Stakes (L), Midsummer Sprint Stakes (L), Woodlands Stakes (L), Cork Stakes (L), Grand Prix Anjou Bretagne (L), Prix Ridgway (L)
Standing in 2019: Haras de la Croix Sonnet, France
Fee in 2019: €1,700
Stallions by his sire include: Makfi (Gr1), Poet's Voice (Gr1), Al Kazeem (L), Akeed Mofeed (winners), Monterosso (winners), Universal (winners), Waldpark (winners), Wilful Default (winners), Worthadd (winners), Hunter's Light (2yo), Night Of Thunder (2yo), Red Dubawi (2yo), Willow Magic (2yo), New Bay (yearlings), Dartmouth (foals), Erupt (foals), Postponed (foals), Time Test (foals), Zarak (foals)

RED DUBAWI (IRE) – chestnut 2008

Dubawi (IRE)	Dubai Millennium (GB)	Seeking The Gold (USA)
		Colorado Dancer
	Zomaradah (GB)	Deploy
		Jawaher (IRE)
Maredsous (FR)	Homme De Loi (IRE)	Law Society (USA)
		Our Village
	Tutti (FR)	Rahotep (FR)
		Flor De Oro (FR)

SALES YEARLINGS OF 2018

Sold in Euros

Nour Dubawi (FR) — bf - Zuckerpuppe (by Seattle Dancer) - BBAG - October - €26,000

Sizeniere (FR) — bf - Sizalia (by Dream Well) - Osarus - September - €24,000

Crush On Me (FR) — bf - Abbreviator (by Astronomer Royal) - Arqana - October - €10,000

Red Confiture (FR) — chf - Lady Marmalade (by Hurricane Run) - Arqana - November - €7,000

Saint Dubawi (FR) — bg - Kermeline (by Le Balafre) - Osarus - November - €5,000

Chc - Louisiane (by Barastraight) - Arqana - November - €4,000

Not Sold

Bc - Eau Et Sable (by Lando) - Arqana - November

Ken Red (FR) — bc - Kendra (by Goofalik) - BBAG - October

SHOOTING TO WIN (AUS)

A full-brother to Group 2-winning sprinter Deep Field – whose first-crop juvenile son Cosmic Force ran away with the Group 3 Pago Pago Stakes over six furlongs at Rosehill in mid-March – the Australian-bred mile Group 1 star Shooting To Win stood one season at Kildangan Stud but covered only 35 mares, resulting in 24 foals. The Darley team member is a son of the late six-furlong Group 1 winner Northern Meteor (by Encosta De Lago) and so is a grandson of Fairy King (by Northern Dancer).

He is out of three-time winner Listen Here (by Elusive Quality), and his unraced grandam, Announce (by Military Plume), is a half-sister to Group 1 scorer Emerald Dream (by Danehill). Third dam Theme Song (by Sackford) won twice but is a half-sister to Group 1 star Danewin (by Danehill) and pattern-winning sprinter Commands (by Danehill), both of whom excelled as stallions. This means that the fourth dam of Shooting To Win is Cotehele House (by My Swanee), an unraced daughter of the phenomenal broodmare Eight Carat (by Pieces Of Eight). The half-sister to European Group 1 sprint star Habibti (by Habitat) produced a record five Group 1 winners at stud, including multimillionaire and leading sire Octagonal (by Zabeel).

With family connections like these, it will be a surprise if Shooting To Win fails to get some Group 1 performers in the southern hemisphere where his first juveniles include a Group 3-placed colt. How his small European crop fares will be interesting, but likely less notable. That said, it would be no surprise to see at least one or two of them do well here. He looks likely to get winners in all age groups, with his best proving effective in the six-to-12-furlong range.

SUMMARY DETAILS

Stood in 2016: Kildangan Stud, Ireland
Fee in 2016: €7,000
Career highlights: 4 wins inc Caulfield Guineas (Gr1), Stan Fox Stakes (Gr2), 2nd Ming Dynasty Quality (Gr3), 3rd Randwick Guineas (Gr1), Golden Rose Stakes (Gr1)
Standing in 2019: in Australia
Stallions by his sire include: Zoustar (Gr1), Deep Field (Gr3), Eurozone (L), Fighting Sun (L), Shooting To Win (winners)

SHOOTING TO WIN (AUS) – chestnut 2011

Northern Meteor (AUS)	Encosta De Lago (AUS)	Fairy King (USA)
		Shoal Creek (AUS)
	Explosive (USA)	Fappiano (USA)
		Scuff (USA)
Listen Here (AUS)	Elusive Quality (USA)	Gone West (USA)
		Touch Of Greatness (USA)
	Announce (AUS)	Military Plume (NZ)
		Theme Song (NZ)

SALES YEARLINGS OF 2018

Sold in Euros

Angel Lucky (IRE)

chc - Infinity (by Bering) - Tatts IRE - September - €15,000
bf - Pixie Belle (by Echo Of Light) - Goffs - November - €8,000
bc - Zakhrafa (by Shamardal) - Tatts IRE - September - €7,500
chf - Gaby (by Aussie Rules) - SGA - September - €5,000
chc - Zoudie (by Ezzoud) - Goffs - November - €4,000
chc - Varna (by Efisio) - Tatts IRE - September - €3,000
chc - Shahralasal (by Oasis Dream) - Goffs - November - €1,500
chf - Cuca Vela (by Devil's Bag) - Tatts IRE - September - €1,000 (p/s)
chc - Spirit Of Success (by Invincible Spirit) - Goffs - February - €1,000

Sold in Guineas

bc - Jillanar (by Lawman) - Tattersalls - October - 7,000gns

Sold in Pounds

Greyfire (GB)

grc - Ancestral Way (by Mtoto) - Tatts IRE Ascot - September - £30,000
bf - Ellikan (by Exceed And Excel) - Goffs UK - August - £16,000

196

chc - Spirit Of Success (by Invincible
Spirit) - Goffs UK - August - £2,000

Not Sold (inc. vendor buy-backs)

chf - Bronze Queen (by Invincible
Spirit) - Goffs - October
bc - Kerimpour (by Marju) - Goffs -
November
bc - Marju Lass (by Marju) - Tatts IRE
Ascot - September
chc - Shalamzara (by Tiger Hill) - Goffs
- November
chf - Sweet Kristeen (by Candy Stripes)
- Goffs - November
chf - Zoumie (by Mark Of Esteem) -
Goffs - November

SIDESTEP (AUS)

The top two-year-old colt in Australia following a six-furlong Group 2 success and a second-place finish in the Group 1 Golden Slipper Stakes, Sidestep (by Exceed And Excel) was also a Group 2-winning sprinter at three, and he shuttles to Haras du Logis. There were 61 foals in his first French crop.

He is by the sire of somewhat successful young stallions Excelebration and Helmet – both of whom have a Group 1 star to their names – the southern hemisphere half of his first crop has produced a Group 1 winner and potential champion, and he is out one of three notable offspring of mile Group 2 scorer Dextrous (by Quest For Fame). Those two siblings are also at stud, they are both by Commands (by Danehill), and they are Group 1 scorer Skilled and Group 1-placed Group 2-winning sprinter Ambidexter. Dextrous is a half-sister to Group 1 AJC Oaks runner-up Light Work (by Danehill), she is out of Group 3-placed Many Hands (by Handy Proverb), and the next dam is an unraced half-sister to dual Australian champion and prolific Group 1 star Emancipation (by Bletchingly).

In addition to being a standout on the track, Emancipation also made an impact at stud. Group 2 scorer and Group 1 AJC Derby runner-up Royal Pardon (by Vice Regal) was her best runner, but her many stakes-winning descendants include the Group 1 scorers Stratum Star (by Stratum), Virage De Fortune (by Anabaa), Rumya (by Red Ransom), and Railings (by Zabeel).

Sidestep is likely to get high-class two-year-olds plus three-year-olds and older horses who prove best as sprinters or milers, with some who stay a bit farther. It will be interesting to see how his European stock fare. His first Australian juveniles have already yielded Godolphin's homebred filly and likely juvenile champion Kiamichi who won the Group 3 Harrolds Magic Night Stakes over six furlongs at Rosehill in mid-March before adding the Group 1 Longines Golden Slipper on soft, over the course and distance, a week later. It would be no surprise to see some stakes and pattern winners among Sidestep's runners here too.

SUMMARY DETAILS

Stood in 2016: Haras de Logis, France

Fee in 2016: €4,000
Career highlights: 4 wins inc Pago Pago Stakes (Gr2), Royal Sovereign Stakes (Gr2), Randwick Equine Derby Munro Stakes (L), 2nd Golden Slipper Stakes (Gr1), Black Opal Stakes (L), Xirrus Fireball Quality Handicap (L), 3rd Merson Cooper Stakes (L)
Standing in 2019: in Australia
Stallions by his sire include: Excelebration (Gr1), Helmet (Gr1), Sidestep (Gr1), Bungle Inthejungle (Gr3), Exceedingly Good (Gr3), Burwaaz (winners), Kuroshio (winners), Fulbright (2yo), Outstrip (2yo), Buratino (yearlings), Cotai Glory (foals), James Garfield (new)

SIDESTEP (AUS) – bay 2010

Exceed And Excel (AUS)	Danehill (USA)	Danzig (USA)
		Razyana (USA)
	Patrona (USA)	Lomond (USA)
		Gladiolus (USA)
Dextrous (AUS)	Quest For Fame	Rainbow Quest (USA)
		Aryenne (FR)
	Many Hands (AUS)	Handy Proverb (AUS)
		Deliberation (AUS)

SALES YEARLINGS OF 2018
Sold in Euros

Isine (FR)	bf - Ivory Style (by Desert Style) - Arqana - August - €95,000
Ideal King (FR)	bc - Ideal World (by Singspiel) - Arqana - August - €45,000 (p/s)
	bc - Miss Eva (by Xaar) - Arqana - October - €33,000
Ilyouchkine (FR)	bc - Such A Memory (by Hold That Tiger) - Osarus - September - €27,000
	bc - Shamazing (by Makfi) - Osarus - September - €22,000
	bc - Anavera (by Acatenango) - Arqana - November - €19,000
El Pago Pago (FR)	bc - Lady Calido (by El Prado) - Arqana - October - €18,000
Hejdau (FR)	bc - Lonestar Spirit (by Invincible Spirit) - Osarus - September - €18,000

	bf - Eva Kant (by Medicean) - Arqana - August - €16,000 (p/s)
Wheels On Fire (FR)	bc - Winds Up (by Street Sense) - Arqana - October - €16,000
Eternal Story (FR)	bc - Earth Affair (by Acatenango) - Osarus - September - €15,000
	bc - Pearls Of Wisdom (by Kyllachy) - Goffs - November - €14,000
Autumnal (FR)	bf - Winter Robin (by Three Valleys) - Osarus - September - €13,000
La Rablais (FR)	bf - Next To The Top (by Hurricane Run) - Arqana - October - €12,000 (p/s)
Elsid (FR)	bc - Elusive Kay (by Elusive City) - Arqana - November - €11,000
	bf - Chambles (by Shamardal) - Arqana - November - €10,000
	bc - Rosen Opera (by Rosen Kavalier) - Arqana - November - €7,000
Best Step (FR)	bf - Shawnee's Best (by King's Best) - Osarus - September - €7,000 (p/s)
Assassin (FR)	bc - Jazz Art (by Dynaformer) - Arqana - October - €6,500
My Perfect (FR)	bc - Like It Is (by Kendor) - Osarus - September - €3,000 (p/s)
	bf - Zomorroda (by Chineur) - BBAG - October - €2,000

Sold in Guineas

bc - Question (by Coronado's Quest) - Tattersalls - October - 32,000gns

brf - Artistica (by Spectrum) - Tattersalls - October - 8,000gns

Sold in Pounds

bc - Cheap N Chic (by Primo Valentino) - Goffs UK - October - £50,000

Not Sold (inc. vendor buy-backs)

Akatino (GER)	bc - Akatina (by Desert Prince) - Baden-Baden - August
Liez (FR)	bc - Elusive Feeling (by Elusive Quality) - Osarus - September
Elsid (FR)	bc - Elusive Kay (by Elusive City) - Arqana - August
	bc - Love Aloft (by Lope De Vega) - Arqana - August
Niagaras Power (GER)	brf - Nightdance Sun (by Monsun) - BBAG - October
	bf - Queen To Be (by King's Best) - Arqana - October
Robinson (FR)	bc - Rose Of Logis (by Slickly) - Osarus - September
Seven Songs (FR)	bc - Seventh Sense (by Samum) - Baden-Baden - August
Steve Malpic (FR)	bc - Simla Snow (by Rock Of Gibraltar) - Osarus - September
	bc - Utopia Jem (by Okawango) - Osarus - September

SUPPLICANT (GB)

A tiny first crop for this talented son of Kyllachy (by Pivotal), with six registered in his first crop and nine, so far, in his second. His first season was at Petches Farm in Essex, and he moved to France after that. He is now at Haras des Trois Chapelles.

Supplicant won the Group 2 Mill Reef Stakes and Listed Ripon Champion Trophy, he was runner-up in the Listed Windsor Castle Stakes, and he is a full-brother to Penitent, winner of the Group 2 Bet365 Mile and Group 2 Joel Stakes and runner-up in the Group 1 Prix de la Foret. The pair are among 11 winners out of two-time scorer Pious (by Bishop Of Cashel), a daughter of Group 3 Princess Margeret Stakes third La Cabrilla (by Carwhite). That mare was out of triple winner La Tuerta (by Hot Spark) which made her a half-sister to the Group 1 Nunthorpe Stakes dead-heater Ya Malak (by Fairy King).

La Tuerta is also the dam of Dominio (by Dominion), who won the Listed St Hugh's Stakes and was second in the Group 2 Temple Stakes before going on to produce Group 2 King's Stand Stakes heroine Dominica (by Alhaarth), and that speedy filly is also the ancestor of a string of blacktype winners, notably the Group 1 Cheveley Park Stakes-placed, pattern-winning pair Rimth (by Oasis Dream) and Kiyoshi (by Dubawi).

But what makes Supplicant an interesting member of the stallion ranks is that La Tuerta was out of Group 3 Temple Stakes winner Smarten Up (by Sharpen Up) which made her a half-sister to Cadeaux Genereux (by Young Generation). He won the Group 1 July Cup and Group 1 William Hill Sprint Championship (previously and since the Nunthorpe Stakes), he was third in the Group 1 Prix du Moulin de Longchamp, and went on to become a notably successful sire whose tally of 64 stakes winners featured eight who won at least once at the highest level.

Kyllachy's handful of stallion sons includes blacktype sire Dragon Pulse and the busy Cheveley Park Stud resident Twilight Son whose first foals were very popular in the auction ring in 2018. It will be interesting to see how Supplicant's career turns out, and it would be no surprise to see him get at least one blacktype horse among a collection of sprint and mile handicappers.

SUMMARY DETAILS

Stood in 2016: Petches Farm, England
Fee in 2016: £3,000
Career highlights: 4 wins inc Mill Reef Stakes (Gr2), Ripon Champion Trophy (L), 2nd Windsor Castle Stakes (L)
Standing in 2019: Haras des Trois Chapelles, France
Fee in 2019: €3,000
Stallions by his sire include: Dragon Pulse (Gr3), Arabian Gleam (winners), Tariq (winners), Supplicant (2yo), Twilight Son (yearlings)

SUPPLICANT (GB) – bay 2011

Kyllachy (GB)	Pivotal (GB)	Polar Falcon (USA)
		Fearless Revival
	Pretty Poppy (GB)	Song
		Moonlight Serenade
Pious (GB)	Bishop Of Cashel (GB)	Warning
		Ballet Classique (USA)
	La Cabrilla	Carwhite
		La Tuerta

SALES YEARLINGS OF 2018

Sold in Euros

Baileys Revalation (FR)	bf - Golbahar (by Holy Roman Emperor) - Arqana - August - €15,000
	bf - Jalissa (by Mister Baileys) - Osarus - September - €15,000
	bc - My Inspiration (by Invincible Spirit) - Arqana - August - €14,000

TELESCOPE (IRE)

Sadler's Wells (by Northern Dancer) has had a phenomenal effect on both the flat and National Hunt racing and breeding sectors and his brilliant son and prolific champion sire Galileo appears to be following suit. He already has a double-digit tally of sons who have at least one top-level flat winner somewhere in the world and a growing number of sons who are making an impact or being aimed at the National Hunt market. Timeform 127-rated Telescope is among the latter.

The Shade Oak Stud stallion was a top-class middle-distance horse, his dam, Velouette (by Darshaan), is an unraced half-sister to Group 1 Dubai World Cup star Moon Ballad (by Singspiel), and his grandam is Velvet Moon (by Shaadi), a Group 2 Lowther Stakes-winning half-sister to Group 1 Derby Italiano winner and Group 1 Melbourne Cup runner-up Central Park (by In The Wings). That horse's full-sister Mellow Park won the Group 3 Lancashire Oaks, and their dam's siblings included Group 3 Horris Hill Stakes winner Gouriev (by Gorytus) and dual Irish Group 3 scorer Careafolie (by Caerleon).

It seems unlikely that Telescope will have many – if any – runners on the flat, so it may be some time before we begin to see what his offspring can do. He has the potential to become a leading British-based National Hunt sire. His initial book yielded 90 foals.

SUMMARY DETAILS

Stood in 2016: Shade Oak Stud, England
Fee in 2016: £3,000
Career highlights: 5 wins inc Hardwicke Stakes (Gr2), Great Voltigeur Stakes (Gr2), Aston Park Stakes (L), 2nd King George VI and Queen Elizabeth Stakes (Gr1), Jockey Club Stakes (Gr2), Rose of Lancaster Stakes (Gr3), Gordon Richards Stakes (Gr3), Huxley Stakes (Gr3), 3rd Juddmonte International Stakes (Gr1)
Standing in 2019: Shade Oak Stud, England
Fee in 2019: £3,000
Stallions by his sire include: Cima De Triomphe (Gr1), Frankel (Gr1), Heliostatic (Gr1), Intello (Gr1), Nathaniel (Gr1), New Approach (Gr1), Rip Van Winkle (Gr1), Roderic O'Connor

(Gr1), Ruler Of The World (Gr1), Sixties Icon (Gr1), Soldier Of Fortune (Gr1), Teofilo (Gr1), Treasure Beach (Gr1)

TELESCOPE (IRE) – bay 2010

Galileo (IRE)	Sadler's Wells (USA)	Northern Dancer (CAN)	
		Fairy Bridge (USA)	
	Urban Sea (USA)	Miswaki (USA)	
		Allegretta	
Velouette (GB)	Darshaan	Shirley Heights	
		Delsy (FR)	
	Velvet Moon (IRE)	Shaadi (USA)	
		Park Special	

SALES YEARLINGS OF 2018

Sold in Euros

bg - Miss Chinchilla (by Perpendicular) - Tatts IRE - November - €14,000

Sold in Pounds

bc - Theatre Belle (by King's Theatre) - Goffs UK - January - £21,000
bc - Tally Em Up (by Flemensfirth) - Goffs UK - January - £16,000
bc - Mi Money (by Alflora) - Goffs UK - January - £12,000
bc - Little Carmela (by Beat Hollow) - Goffs UK - January - £10,000
bc - Rattlin (by Bollin Eric) - Goffs UK - January - £10,000
bc - Fragrant Rose (by Alflora) - Goffs UK - January - £8,000
bc - Kahooting (by Kahyasi) - Goffs UK - January - £8,000
bf - Ancora (by Accordion) - Goffs UK - January - £6,000
bc - Tiger Line (by Kayf Tara) - Goffs UK - January - £5,000 (p/s)
bc - Libritish (by Librettist) - Goffs UK - January - £4,500
bc - Linagram (by Classic Cliche) - Goffs UK - January - £3,500

bc - Pougatcheva (by Epervier Bleu) - Goffs UK - January - £3,000
bc - Florarossa (by Alflora) - Tatts IRE - February - €2,000
bf - Let It Be (by Entrepreneur) - Goffs UK - January - £2,000
bf - En Reve (by Shirocco) - Goffs UK - January - £1,200
bf - Precious Lady (by Exit To Nowhere) - Goffs UK - January - £800

Not Sold (inc. vendor buy-backs)

bg - Bestow (by Presenting) - Tatts IRE - November
bc - Lady In The Bath (by Forzando) - Goffs - February
bc - Laetitia (by Priolo) - Goffs UK - January
blc - Tomitoul Star (by Dansili) - Goffs UK - January

THE WOW SIGNAL (IRE)

Star sprinter Starspangledbanner (by Choisir) had small early crops, due to much-publicised fertility issues, but his first batch featured leading European juvenile The Wow Signal.

The colt burst on to the scene with a nine-length debut score over six furlongs at Ayr in late May, followed-up by beating Cappella Sansevero by one and three-quarter lengths in the Group 2 Coventry Stakes at Royal Ascot, and then beat Hootenanny by half a length to secure the Group 1 Prix Morny at Deauville. He was unplaced on his only other start, ended the year on a Timeform rating of 118, and eventually took up stallion duties at Haras de Bouquetot in Normandy. Sadly, there are just nine in his first crop, and he died in March 2018.

A half-brother to seven-furlong listed scorer and Group 2 Rockfel Stakes third Miss Infinity (by Rock Of Gibraltar), he was out of Muravka (by High Chaparral), a half-sister to dual stakes-winning miler Tolpuddle (by College Chapel). Grandam Tabdea (by Topsider) won a mile listed contest at Doncaster and was third in the Group 2 Prix de l'Opera over nine furlongs, and she was a half-sister to Group 1 Poule d'Essai des Pouliches (French 1000 Guineas) heroine Ta Rib (by Mr Prospector).

The small number progeny he left behind likely include sprinters and milers, and it would be no surprise if at least one or two of them become a blacktype horse or even a pattern winner.

SUMMARY DETAILS

Stood in 2016: Haras de Bouquetot, France
Fee in 2016: €8,000
Career highlights: 3 wins inc Prix Morny (Gr1), Coventry Stakes (Gr2)
Standing in 2019: died in 2018
Stallions by his sire include: The Wow Signal (2yo)

THE WOW SIGNAL (IRE) – bay 2012

Starspangledbanner (AUS)	Choisir (AUS)	Danehill Dancer (IRE)
		Great Selection (AUS)
	Gold Anthem (AUS)	Made Of Gold (USA)
		National Song (AUS)
Muravka (IRE)	High Chaparral (IRE)	Sadler's Wells (USA)
		Kasora (IRE)
	Tabdea (USA)	Topsider (USA)
		Madame Secretary (USA)

SALES YEARLINGS OF 2018
Sold in Euros

	bf - Sister Golightly (by Mtoto) - Arqana - August - €100,000
Disincanto (FR)	chf - Lady Sadowa (by Nayef) - Osarus - September - €35,000
	chf - Storia Dell'Isola (by Vespone) - Osarus - September - €22,000
Space Ace (FR)	chf - Imperial Topaz (by Dutch Art) - Arqana - August - €20,000

Sold in Pounds

bc - Chickasaw (by Bertolini) - Goffs UK - August - £32,000

FRESHMAN SIRES OF 2019
BY STUD IN 2016
(2019 IN BRACKETS, IF DIFFERENT)

Ireland

Ballylinch Stud – Make Believe (GB)

Bridge House Stud – Cappella Sansevero (GB)

Castlehyde Stud – Ivawood (IRE)
Castlehyde Stud – Kingston Hill (GB)

Coolmore Stud – Gleneagles (IRE)

Garryrichard Stud – Hillstar (GB)

Irish National Stud – Free Eagle (IRE)

Kildangan Stud – French Navy (GB)
Kildangan Stud – Fulbright (GB)
Kildangan Stud (in Australia) – Hallowed Crown (AUS)
Kildangan Stud (Dalham Hall Stud, England) – Night Of
    Thunder (IRE)
Kildangan Stud (in Australia) – Shooting To Win (AUS)

Rathasker Stud – Anjaal (GB)

Sunnyhill Stud – Lucky Speed (IRE)

Tally-Ho Stud (withdrawn) – G Force (IRE)

Windmill View Stud – Gatewood (GB)

Yeomanstown Stud – Gutaifan (IRE)

United Kingdom

Bearstone Stud – Fountain Of Youth (IRE)

Dalham Hall Stud – Brazen Beau (AUS)

Dalham Hall Stud – Golden Horn (GB)
Dalham Hall Stud – Outstrip (GB)

Hedgeholme Stud – Intrinsic (GB)

Highclere Stud – Cable Bay (IRE)

Nunnery Stud – Muhaarar (GB)

Overbury Stud (Haras de Fleury, France) – Mustajeeb (GB)

Petches Farm Stud (Haras des Trois Chapelles, France) –
    Supplicant (GB)

Shade Oak Stud – Telescope (GB)

Throckmorton Court Stud – Music Master (GB)

Tweenhills Farm & Stud – Hot Streak (IRE)

Whitsbury Manor Stud – Due Diligence (USA)

Yorton Farm Stud – Pether's Moon (IRE)

France
Haras de Bouquetot (dead) – The Wow Signal (IRE)

Haras de Colleville – Galiway (GB)

Haras de Grandcamp (in Tunisia) – Evasive's First (FR)

Haras de Logis – Hunter's Light (IRE)
Haras de Logis (in Australia) – Sidestep (AUS)

Haras de la Reboursiere et de Montaigu – Prince Gibraltar (FR)

Haras des Sablonnets (Haras de la Croix Sonnet, France) – Red
    Dubawi (IRE)

Haras du Thenney (Gestut Helenenhof, Germany) – Amarillo (IRE)

Germany
Gestut Etzean – Amaron (GB)

Gestut Helenenhof – Earl Of Tinsdal (GER)

Gestut Lindenhof (Gestut Erftmuhle, Germany) – Nutan (IRE)

United States of America
Ashford Stud – American Pharoah (USA)

Gainesway – Karakontie (JPN)

FRESHMAN SIRES OF 2019
BY FEE IN 2016

Euros

€60,000 – Gleneagles (IRE)

€30,000 – Night Of Thunder (IRE)

€20,000 – Free Eagle (IRE)
€20,000 – Make Believe (GB)

€12,500 – Gutaifan (IRE)

€9,000 – Ivawood (IRE)

€8,000 – G Force (IRE)
€8,000 – The Wow Signal (IRE)

€7,000 – Hallowed Crown (AUS)
€7,000 – Shooting To Win (AUS)

€6,000 – Kingston Hill (GB)

€5,000 – Anjaal (GB)

€4,500 – Amaron (GB)
€4,500 – Cappella Sansevero (GB)

€4,000 – Earl Of Tinsdal (GER)
€4,000 – French Navy (GB)
€4,000 – Fulbright (GB)
€4,000 – Hunter's Light (IRE)
€4,000 – Sidestep (AUS)

€3,500 – Nutan (IRE)

€3,000 – Amarillo (IRE)
€3,000 – Evasive's First (FR)
€3,000 – Galiway (GB)
€3,000 – Prince Gibraltar (FR)

€2,000 – Red Dubawi (IRE)

€1,500 – Gatewood (GB)

on application – Hillstar (GB)
on application – Lucky Speed (IRE)

Pounds
£60,000 – Golden Horn (GB)

£30,000 – Muhaarar (GB)

£10,000 – Brazen Beau (AUS)

£7,000 – Hot Streak (IRE)

£6,500 – Cable Bay (IRE)
£6,500 – Due Diligence (USA)

£5,000 – Fountain Of Youth (IRE)
£5,000 – Mustajeeb (GB)
£5,000 – Outstrip (GB)

£4,000 – Music Master (GB)

£3,000 – Supplicant (GB)
£3,000 – Telescope (GB)

£2,250 – Pether's Moon (IRE)

£1,750 – Intrinsic (GB)

US Dollars
$200,000 – American Pharoah (USA)

$15,000 – Karakontie (JPN)

FRESHMAN SIRES OF 2019
BY SIRE

Bahamian Bounty (GB) – Anjaal (GB)

Bernstein (USA) – Karakontie (JPN)

Black Sam Bellamy (IRE) – Earl Of Tinsdal (GER)

Cape Cross (IRE) – Golden Horn (GB)

Danehill Dancer (IRE) – Hillstar (GB)

Dark Angel (IRE) – Gutaifan (IRE)

Dubawi (IRE) – Hunter's Light (IRE)
Dubawi (IRE) – Night Of Thunder (IRE)
Dubawi (IRE) – Red Dubawi (IRE)

Duke Of Marmalade (IRE) – Nutan (IRE)

Dylan Thomas (IRE) – Pether's Moon (IRE)

Evasive (GB) – Evasive's First (FR)

Exceed And Excel (AUS) – Fulbright (GB)
Exceed And Excel (AUS) – Outstrip (GB)
Exceed And Excel (AUS) – Sidestep (AUS)

Galileo (IRE) – Galiway (GB)
Galileo (IRE) – Gatewood (GB)
Galileo (IRE) – Gleneagles (IRE)
Galileo (IRE) – Telescope (GB)

High Chaparral (IRE) – Free Eagle (IRE)

Holy Roman Emperor (IRE) – Amarillo (IRE)

I Am Invincible (AUS) – Brazen Beau (AUS)

215

FRESHMAN SIRES OF 2019

Iffraaj (GB) – Hot Streak (IRE)

Invincible Spirit (IRE) – Cable Bay (IRE)

Kyllachy (GB) – Supplicant (GB)

Makfi (GB) – Make Believe (GB)

Mastercraftsman (IRE) – Kingston Hill (GB)

Nayef (USA) – Mustajeeb (GB)

Northern Meteor (AUS) – Shooting To Win (AUS)

Oasis Dream (GB) – Fountain Of Youth (IRE)
Oasis Dream (GB) – Intrinsic (GB)
Oasis Dream (GB) – Muhaarar (GB)

Piccolo (GB) – Music Master (GB)

Pioneerof The Nile (USA) – American Pharoah (USA)

Rock Of Gibraltar (IRE) – Prince Gibraltar (FR)

Shamardal (USA) – Amaron (GB)
Shamardal (USA) – French Navy (GB)

Showcasing (GB) – Cappella Sansevero (GB)

Silvano (GER) – Lucky Speed (IRE)

Starspanglesbanner (AUS) – The Wow Signal (IRE)

Street Sense (USA) – Hallowed Crown (AUS)

Tamayuz (GB) – G Force (IRE)

War Front (USA) – Due Diligence (USA)

Zebedee (GB) – Ivawood (IRE)

FRESHMAN SIRES OF 2019
BY GRANDSIRE

Acclamation (GB) – Gutaifan (IRE), by Dark Angel (IRE)

Cadeaux Genereux – Anjaal (GB), by Bahamian Bounty (GB)

Choisir (AUS) – The Wow Signal (IRE), by Starspangledbanner (AUS)

Danehill (USA) – Amarillo (IRE), by Holy Roman Emperor (IRE)
Danehill (USA) – Fulbright (GB), by Exceed And Excel (AUS)
Danehill (USA) – Hillstar (GB), by Danehill Dancer (IRE)
Danehill (USA) – Nutan (IRE), by Duke Of Marmalade (IRE)
Danehill (USA) – Outstrip (GB), by Exceed And Excel (AUS)
Danehill (USA) – Pether's Moon (IRE), by Dylan Thomas (IRE)
Danehill (USA) – Prince Gibraltar (FR), by Rock Of Gibraltar (IRE)
Danehill (USA) – Sidestep (AUS), by Exceed And Excel (AUS)

Danehill Dancer (IRE) – Kingston Hill (GB), by Mastercraftsman (IRE)

Danzig (USA) – Due Diligence (USA), by War Front (USA)

Dubai Millennium (GB) – Hunter's Light (IRE), by Dubawi (IRE)
Dubai Millennium (GB) – Night Of Thunder (IRE), by Dubawi (IRE)
Dubai Millennium (GB) – Red Dubawi (IRE), by Dubawi (IRE)

Dubawi (IRE) – Make Believe (GB), by Makfi (GB)

Elusive Quality (USA) – Evasive's First (FR), by Evasive (GB)

Empire Maker (USA) – American Pharoah (USA), by Pioneerof The Nile (USA)

Encosta De Lago (AUS) – Shooting To Win (AUS), by Northern
    Meteor (AUS)

Giant's Causeway (USA) – Amaron (GB), by Shamardal (GB)
Giant's Causeway (USA) – French Navy (GB), by Shamardal
    (GB)

Green Desert (USA) – Cable Bay (IRE), by Invincible Spirit
    (IRE)
Green Desert (USA) – Fountain Of Youth (IRE), by Oasis
    Dream (GB)
Green Desert (USA) – Golden Horn (GB), by Cape Cross (IRE)
Green Desert (USA) – Intrinsic (GB), by Oasis Dream (GB)
Green Desert (USA) – Muhaarar (GB), by Oasis Dream (GB)

Gulch (USA) – Mustajeeb (GB), by Nayef (USA)

Invincible Spirit (IRE) – Brazen Beau (AUS), by I Am Invincible
    (AUS)
Invincible Spirit (IRE) – Ivawood (IRE), by Zebedee (GB)

Lomitas (GB) – Lucky Speed (IRE), by Silvano (GER)

Nayef (USA) – G Force (IRE), by Tamayuz (GB)

Oasis Dream (GB) – Cappella Sansevero (GB), by Showcasing
    (GB)

Pivotal (GB) – Supplicant (GB), by Kyllachy (GB)

Sadler's Wells (USA) – Earl Of Tinsdal (GER), by Black Sam
    Bellamy (IRE)
Sadler's Wells (USA) – Free Eagle (IRE), by High Chaparral
    (IRE)
Sadler's Wells (USA) – Galiway (GB), by Galileo (IRE)
Sadler's Wells (USA) – Gatewood (GB), by Galileo (IRE)
Sadler's Wells (USA) – Gleneagles (IRE), by Galileo (IRE)
Sadler's Wells (USA) – Telescope (GB), by Galileo (IRE)

Storm Cat (USA) – Karakontie (JPN), by Bernstein (USA)

Street Cry (IRE) – Hallowed Crown (AUS), by Street Sense (USA)

Warning – Music Master (GB), by Piccolo (GB)

Zafonic (USA) – Hot Streak (IRE), by Iffraaj (GB)

FRESHMAN SIRES OF 2019
BY GREAT-GRANDSIRE

Danehill (USA) – Kingston Hill (GB), by Mastercraftsman (IRE), by Danehill Dancer (IRE)

Danehill Dancer (IRE) – The Wow Signal (IRE), by Starspangledbanner (AUS), by Choisir (AUS)

Danzig (USA) – Amarillo (IRE), by Holy Roman Emperor (IRE), by Danehill (USA)

Danzig (USA) – Cable Bay (IRE), by Invincible Spirit (IRE), by Green Desert (USA)

Danzig (USA) – Fountain Of Youth (IRE), by Oasis Dream (GB), by Green Desert (USA)

Danzig (USA) – Fulbright (GB), by Exceed And Excel (AUS), by Danehill (USA)

Danzig (USA) – Golden Horn (GB), by Cape Cross (IRE), by Green Desert (USA)

Danzig (USA) – Hillstar (GB), by Danehill Dancer (IRE), by Danehill (USA)

Danzig (USA) – Intrinsic (GB), by Oasis Dream (GB), by Green Desert (USA)

Danzig (USA) – Muhaarar (GB), by Oasis Dream (GB), by Green Desert (USA)

Danzig (USA) – Nutan (IRE), by Duke Of Marmalade (IRE), by Danehill (USA)

Danzig (USA) – Outstrip (GB), by Exceed And Excel (AUS), by Danehill (USA)

Danzig (USA) – Pether's Moon (IRE), by Dylan Thomas (IRE), by Danehill (USA)

Danzig (USA) – Prince Gibraltar (FR), by Rock Of Gibraltar (IRE), by Danehill (USA)

Danzig (USA) – Sidestep (AUS), by Exceed And Excel (AUS), by Danehill (USA)

Dubai Millennium (GB) – Make Believe (GB), by Makfi (GB), by Dubawi (IRE)

Fairy King (USA) – Shooting To Win (AUS), by Northern
Meteor (AUS), by Encosta De Lago (AUS)

Gone West (USA) – Evasive's First (FR), by Evasive (GB), by
Elusive Quality (USA)
Gone West (USA) – Hot Streak (IRE), by Iffraaj (GB), by
Zafonic (USA)

Green Desert (USA) – Brazen Beau (AUS), by I Am Invincible
(AUS), by Invincible Spirit (IRE)
Green Desert (USA) – Cappella Sansevero (GB), by Showcasing
(GB), by Oasis Dream (GB)
Green Desert (USA) – Ivawood (IRE), by Zebedee (GB), by
Invincible Spirit (IRE)

Gulch (USA) – G Force (IRE), by Tamayuz (GB), by Nayef
(USA)

Known Fact (USA) – Music Master (GB), by Piccolo (GB), by
Warning

Machiavellian (USA) – Hallowed Crown (AUS), by Street Sense
(USA)

Mr Prospector (USA) – Mustajeeb (GB), by Nayef (USA), by
Gulch (USA)

Niniski (USA) – Lucky Speed (IRE), by Silvano (GER), by
Lomitas (GB)

Northern Dancer (CAN) – Due Diligence (USA), by War Front
(USA), by Danzig (USA)
Northern Dancer (CAN) – Earl Of Tinsdal (GER), by Black Sam
Bellamy (IRE), by Sadler's Wells (USA)
Northern Dancer (CAN) – Free Eagle (IRE), by High Chaparral
(IRE), by Sadler's Wells (USA)
Northern Dancer (CAN) – Galiway (GB), by Galileo (IRE), by
Sadler's Wells (USA)
Northern Dancer (CAN) – Gatewood (GB), by Galileo (IRE), by
Sadler's Wells (USA)

Northern Dancer (CAN) – Gleneagles (IRE), by Galileo (IRE),
    by Sadler's Wells (USA)
Northern Dancer (CAN) – Telescope (GB), by Galileo (IRE), by
    Sadler's Wells (USA)

Polar Falcon (USA) – Supplicant (GB), by Kyllachy (GB), by
    Pivotal (GB)

Royal Applause (GB) – Gutaifan (IRE), by Dark Angel (IRE), by
    Acclamation (GB)

Seeking The Gold (USA) – Hunter's Light (IRE), by Dubawi
    (IRE), by Dubai Millennium (GB)
Seeking The Gold (USA) – Night Of Thunder (IRE), by Dubawi
    (IRE), by Dubai Millennium (GB)
Seeking The Gold (USA) – Red Dubawi (IRE), by Dubawi (IRE),
    by Dubai Millennium (GB)

Storm Bird (CAN) – Karakontie (JPN), by Bernstein (USA), by
    Storm Cat (USA)

Storm Cat (USA) – Amaron (GB), by Shamardal (USA), by
    Giant's Causeway (USA)
Storm Cat (USA) – French Navy (GB), by Shamardal (USA), by
    Giant's Causeway (USA)

Unbridled (USA) – American Pharoah (USA), by Pioneerof The
    Nile (USA), by Empire Maker (USA)

Young Generation – Anjaal (GB), by Bahamian Bounty (GB), by
    Cadeaux Genereux

FRESHMAN SIRES OF 2019
BY BROODMARE SIRE

Barathea (IRE) – Hunter's Light (IRE), by Dubawi (IRE)

Bertolini (USA) – Amaron (GB), by Shamardal (USA)

Bin Ajwaad (IRE) – Music Master (GB), by Piccolo (GB)

Bishop Of Cashel (GB) – Supplicant (GB), by Kyllachy (GB)

Common Grounds – G Force (IRE), by Tamayuz (GB)

Danehill (USA) – Free Eagle (IRE), by High Chaparral (IRE)
Danehill (USA) – Galiway (GB), by Galileo (IRE)
Danehill (USA) – Hallowed Crown (AUS), by Street Sense (USA)

Darshaan – Telescope (GB), by Galileo (IRE)

Dashing Blade – Earl Of Tinsdal (GER)

Diktat (GB) – Cable Bay (IRE), by Invincible Spirit (IRE)

Dubai Destination (USA) – Golden Horn (GB), by Cape Cross
(IRE)

Efisio – Fountain Of Youth (IRE), by Oasis Dream (GB)

El Prado (IRE) – Outstrip (GB), by Exceed And Excel (AUS)

Elusive Quality (USA) – Mustajeeb (GB), by Nayef (USA)
Elusive Quality (USA) – Shooting To Win (AUS), by Northern
Meteor (AUS)

Fairy King (USA) – Fulbright (GB), by Exceed And Excel (AUS)

Galileo (IRE) – Night Of Thunder (IRE), by Dubawi (IRE)

High Chaparral (IRE) – The Wow Signal (IRE), by
Starspangledbanner (AUS)

FRESHMAN SIRES OF 2019

Homme De Loi (IRE) – Red Dubawi (IRE), by Dubawi (IRE)

Housebuster (USA) – Hot Streak (IRE), by Iffraaj (GB)

Lahib (USA) – Gutaifan (IRE), by Dark Angel (IRE)

Linamix (FR) – Muhaarar (GB), by Oasis Dream (GB)

Mark Of Esteem (IRE) – Hillstar (GB), by Danehill Dancer (IRE)

Monsun (GER) – Lucky Speed (IRE), by Silvano (GER)

Oasis Dream (GB) – Evasive's First (FR), by Evasive (GB)

Peintre Celebre (USA) – Anjaal (GB), by Bahamian Bounty (GB)
Peintre Celebre (USA) – Nutan (IRE), by Duke Of Marmalade (IRE)

Pennekamp (USA) – Prince Gibraltar (FR), by Rock Of Gibraltar (IRE)

Pivotal (GB) – Intrinsic (GB), by Oasis Dream (GB)

Pulpit (USA) – Due Diligence (USA), by War Front (USA)

Quest For Fame – Sidestep (AUS), by Exceed And Excel (AUS)

Rainbow Quest (USA) – Kingston Hill (GB), by Mastercraftsman (IRE)

Red Ransom (USA) – Ivawood (IRE), by Zebedee (GB)

Royal Academy (USA) – Amarillo (IRE), by Holy Roman Emperor (IRE)

Royal Applause (GB) – Cappella Sansevero (GB), by Showcasing (GB)

Suave Dancer (USA) – Make Believe (GB), by Makfi (GB)

224

Selkirk (USA) – Gatewood (GB), by Galileo (IRE)

Snaadee (USA) – Brazen Beau (AUS), by I Am Invincible (AUS)

Storm Cat (USA) – Gleneagles (IRE), by Galileo (IRE)

Sunday Silence (USA) – Karakontie (JPN), by Bernstein (USA)

Tirol (IRE) – Pether's Moon (IRE), by Dylan Thomas (IRE)

Woodman (USA) – French Navy (GB), by Shamardal (USA)

Yankee Gentleman (USA) – American Pharoah (USA), by
    Pioneerof The Nile (USA)

FRESHMAN SIRES OF 2019
BY DATE OF EARLIEST WIN

February
05 - Brazen Beau (AUS) - 5.5f maiden on good at Canterbury
Park, Australia - 2yo

March
26 - Hallowed Crown (AUS) - 5.75f maiden on soft at
Kensington, Australia - 2yo
30 - Sidestep (AUS) - 6f Group 2 on good at Rosehill, Australia -
2yo

April
01 - Lucky Speed (IRE) - 9.25f newcomers on good-to-soft at
Cologne, Germany - 3yo
16 - Cappella Sansevero (GB) - 5f maiden on standard at
Dundalk, Ireland - 2yo
17 - Music Master (GB) - 7f maiden on good at Newmarket,
England - 3yo
23 - Pether's Moon (IRE) - 1m maiden on standard at Kempton,
England - 3yo
24 - G Force (IRE) - 5f maiden on good at Newcastle, England -
3yo

May
10 - Nutan (IRE) - 11f maiden on good at Cologne, Germany -
3yo
12 - Muhaarar (GB) - 5.5f maiden on soft at Doncaster, England -
2yo
14 - Supplicant (GB) - 5f maiden on good-to-firm at Beverley,
England - 2yo
20 - Fulbright (GB) - 5f maiden on good at Musselburgh,
Scotland - 2yo
21 - Red Dubawi (IRE) - 1m maiden on good at Maisons-Laffitte,
France - 3yo
21 - The Wow Signal (IRE) - 6f maiden on good-to-soft at Ayr,
Scotland - 2yo
27 - Hunter's Light (IRE) - 10f maiden on good at Newmarket,
England - 3yo

29 - Shooting To Win (AUS) - 6f maiden on good at Kembla Grange, Australia - 2yo

June

03 - Cable Bay (IRE) - 6f maiden on good at Leicester, England - 2yo

06 - Fountain Of Youth (IRE) - 5f maiden on good-to-firm at Tipperary, Ireland - 2yo

08 - Anjaal (GB) - 5f maiden on good-to-firm at Beverley, England - 2yo

09 - Evasive's First (FR) - 6.5f conditions on standard at Marseille Pont-de-Vivaux, France - 2yo

13 - Ivawood (IRE) - 5f maiden on good at Sandown, England - 2yo

14 - Gutaifan (IRE) - 6f maiden on good-to-firm at Salisbury, England - 2yo

22 - Outstrip (GB) - 7f maiden on good at Newmarket, England - 2yo

26 - Gatewood (GB) - 10f maiden on good-to-firm at Salisbury, England - 3yo

29 - Gleneagles (IRE) - 7f maiden on good-to-firm at Curragh, Ireland - 2yo

July

01 - Karakontie (JPN) - 7f newcomers on very soft at Compiegne, France - 2yo

09 - Amarillo (IRE) - 7f on good at Dusseldorf, Germany - 2yo

24 - Amaron (GB) - 7f listed race on soft at Cologne, Germany - 2yo

27 - Hot Streak (IRE) - 6f maiden on good-to-firm at York, England - 2yo

29 - Mustajeeb (GB) - 7f maiden on yielding at Galway, Ireland - 2yo

August

10 - French Navy (GB) - 1m newcomers on good at Deauville, France - 2yo

12 - Due Diligence (USA) - 5.5f maiden on firm at Saratoga, USA - 2yo

15 - Free Eagle (IRE) - 1m maiden on good at Leopardstown, Ireland - 2yo

September
04 - American Pharoah (USA) - 7f Grade 1 on fast at Del Mar, USA - 2yo
21 - Kingston Hill (GB) - 7f maiden on soft at Newbury, England - 2yo
26 - Prince Gibraltar (FR) - 1m maiden on good at Maisons-Laffitte, France - 2yo
27 - Galiway (GB) - 1m newcomers on soft at Saint-Cloud, France - 2yo
27 - Telescope (GB) - 1m maiden on good at Newmarket, England - 2yo

October
02 - Intrinsic (GB) - 6f maiden on good-to-firm at Newcastle, England - 3yo
03 - Earl Of Tinsdal (GER) - 1m conditions on soft at Munich, Germany - 2yo
13 - Night Of Thunder (IRE) - 6f maiden on soft at Goodwood, England - 2yo
16 - Hillstar (GB) - 7f maiden on soft at Leicester, England, 2yo
23 - Make Believe (GB) - 7.5f newcomers on soft at Deauville, France - 2yo
29 - Golden Horn (GB) - 8.5f maiden on good-to-soft at Nottingham, England - 2yo

FRESHMAN SIRES OF 2019
BY HIGHEST WIN LEVEL

Group 1 winners
Amaron (GB)
American Pharoah (USA)
Brazen Beau (AUS)
Earl Of Tinsdal (GER)
Free Eagle (IRE)
G Force (IRE)
Gleneagles (IRE)
Golden Horn (GB)
Hallowed Crown (AUS)
Hillstar (GB)
Hunter's Light (IRE)
Karakontie (JPN)
Kingston Hill (GB)
Lucky Speed (IRE)
Make Believe (GB)
Muhaarar (GB)
Night Of Thunder (IRE)
Nutan (IRE)
Outstrip (GB)
Pether's Moon (IRE)
Prince Gibraltar (FR)
Red Dubawi (IRE)
Shooting To Win (AUS)
The Wow Signal (IRE)

Group 2 winners
Anjaal (GB)
Cable Bay (IRE)
Fulbright (GB)
Gutaifan (IRE)
Hot Streak (IRE)
Ivawood (IRE)
Mustajeeb (GB)
Sidestep (AUS)
Supplicant (GB)
Telescope (GB)

Group 3 winners
Amarillo (IRE)
Cappella Sansevero (GB)
Evasive's First (FR)
Fountain Of Youth (IRE)
French Navy (GB)
Gatewood (GB)
Music Master (GB)

Listed winners
Due Diligence (USA) - 3yo
Galiway (GB) - 3yo

Heritage/Premier Handicap winners
Intrinsic (GB)

FRESHMAN SIRES OF 2019
BY DISTANCE OF GROUP WINS

5f
Fountain Of Youth (IRE) - 3yo
Gutaifan (IRE) - 2yo
Hot Streak (IRE) - 2yo, 3yo

5.5f
Gutaifan (IRE) - 2yo
Hallowed Crown (AUS) - 2yo

6f
Amarillo (IRE) - 5yo
Anjaal (GB) - 2yo
Brazen Beau (AUS) - 2yo, 3yo
Cappella Sansevero (GB) - 2yo
G Force (IRE) - 3yo
Hallowed Crown (AUS) -3yo
Ivawood (IRE) - 2yo
Muhaarar (GB) - 2yo, 3yo
Music Master (GB) - 4yo
Mustajeeb (GB) - 4yo
Sidestep (AUS) - 2yo, 3yo
Supplicant (GB) - 2yo
The Wow Signal (IRE) - 2yo

6.5f
Amarillo (IRE) - 5yo
Muhaarar (GB) - 3yo

7f
Amarillo (IRE) - 2yo, 4yo
Americah Pharoah (USA) - 2yo
Cable Bay (IRE) - 4yo
Fulbright (GB) - 3yo
Gleneagles (IRE) - 2yo
Hallowed Crown (AUS) - 3yo
Karakontie (JPN) - 2yo
Make Believe (GB) - 3yo

Muhaarar (GB) - 2yo
Mustajeeb (GB) - 3yo
Outstrip (GB) - 2yo

7.5f
Shooting To Win (AUS) - 3yo

1m
Amaron (GB) - 3yo, 4yo, 5yo, 6yo
Evasive's First (FR) - 2yo
French Navy (GB) - 2yo
Gleneagles (IRE) - 3yo
Hallowed Crown (AUS) - 3yo
Karakontie (JPN) - 3yo
Kingston Hill (GB) - 2yo
Make Believe (GB) - 3yo
Mustajeeb (GB) - 3yo
Night Of Thunder (IRE) - 3yo, 4yo
Outstrip (GB) - 2yo
Red Dubawi (IRE) - 6yo, 7yo
Shooting To Win (AUS) - 3yo

1m 0.5f
Amaron (GB) - 3yo
American Pharoah (USA) - 2yo, 3yo
French Navy (GB) - 6yo

1m1f
Amaron (GB) - 5yo
American Pharoah (USA) - 3yo
French Navy (GB) - 7yo
Hunter's Light (IRE) - 7yo

1m 1.5f
American Pharoah (USA) - 3yo
Hunter's Light (IRE) - 5yo

1m2f
American Pharoah (USA) - 3yo
Earl Of Tinsdal (GER) - 3yo

Free Eagle (IRE) - 3yo, 4yo
French Navy (GB) - 3yo
Golden Horn (GB) - 3yo
Hunter's Light (IRE) - 4yo, 5yo
Lucky Speed (IRE) - 3yo
Prince Gibraltar (FR) - 2yo, 3yo

1m2.5f

Golden Horn (GB) - 3yo
Hunter's Light (IRE) - 4yo

1m3f

Hillstar (GB) - 4yo

1m4f

American Pharoah (USA) - 3yo
Earl Of Tinsdal (GER) - 3yo, 4yo, 5yo
Gatewood (GB) - 4yo
Golden Horn (GB) - 3yo
Hillstar (GB) - 3yo, 4yo
Lucky Speed (IRE) - 3yo
Nutan (IRE) - 3yo
Pether's Moon (IRE) - 4yo, 5yo
Prince Gibraltar (FR) - 4yo
Telescope (GB) - 3yo, 4yo

1m4.5f

Gatewood (GB) - 6yo

1m5.5f

Lucky Speed (IRE) - 5yo

1m6.5f

Kingston Hill (GB) - 3yo

FRESHMAN SIRES OF 2019
BY AGE OF GROUP WINS

2yo
Amaron (GB)
American Pharoah (USA)
Anjaal (GB)
Brazen Beau (AUS)
Cappella Sansevero (GB)
Evasive's First (FR)
French Navy (GB)
Gleneagles (IRE)
Gutaifan (IRE)
Hallowed Crown (AUS)
Hot Streak (IRE)
Ivawood (IRE)
Karakontie (JPN)
Kingston Hill (GB)
Muhaarar (GB)
Outstrip (GB)
Prince Gibraltar (FR)
Sidestep (AUS)
Supplicant (GB)
The Wow Signal (IRE)

3yo
Amaron (GB)
American Pharoah (USA)
Brazen Beau (AUS)
Earl Of Tinsdal (GER)
Fountain Of Youth (IRE)
Free Eagle (IRE)
French Navy (GB)
Fulbright (GB)
G Force (IRE)
Gleneagles (IRE)
Golden Horn (GB)
Hallowed Crown (AUS)
Hillstar (GB)
Hot Streak (IRE)

Karakontie (JPN)
Kingston Hill (GB)
Lucky Speed (IRE)
Make Believe (GB)
Muhaarar (GB)
Mustajeeb (GB)
Night Of Thunder (IRE)
Nutan (IRE)
Prince Gibraltar (FR)
Shooting To Win (AUS)
Sidestep (AUS)
Telescope (GB)

4yo
Amarillo (IRE)
Amaron (GB)
Cable Bay (IRE)
Earl Of Tinsdal (GER)
Free Eagle (IRE)
Gatewood (GB)
Hillstar (GB)
Hunter's Light (IRE)
Music Master (GB)
Mustajeeb (GB)
Night Of Thunder (IRE)
Pether's Moon (IRE)
Prince Gibraltar (FR)
Telescope (GB)

5yo
Amarillo (IRE)
Amaron (GB)
Earl Of Tinsdal (GER)
Hunter's Light (IRE)
Lucky Speed (IRE)
Pether's Moon (IRE)

6yo
Amaron (GB)
French Navy (GB)

Gatewood (GB)
Red Dubawi (IRE)

7yo
French Navy (GB)
Hunter's Light (IRE)
Red Dubawi (IRE)

FRESHMAN SIRES OF 2019
BY GOING DESCRIPTION FOR GROUP WINS

TURF
Firm
Karakontie (JPN) - 3yo
Lucky Speed (IRE) - 5yo
Outstrip (GB) - 2yo

Good-to-firm
Amarillo (IRE) - 4yo
Anjaal (GB) - 2yo
Fountain Of Youth (IRE) - 3yo
Free Eagle (IRE) - 3yo, 4yo
French Navy (GB) - 7yo
Gleneagles (IRE) - 2yo, 3yo
Golden Horn (GB) - 3yo
Hillstar (GB) - 3yo
Hunter's Light (IRE) - 4yo
Ivawood (IRE) - 2yo
Muhaarar (GB) - 3yo
Night Of Thunder (IRE) - 3yo
Pether's Moon (IRE) - 4yo, 5yo
Telescope (GB) - 3yo, 4yo

Good
Amarillo (IRE) - 5yo
Amaron (GB) - 2yo, 5yo, 6yo
Brazen Beau (AUS) - 2yo, 3yo
Cable Bay (IRE) - 4yo
Earl Of Tinsdal (GER) - 3yo
French Navy (GB) - 6yo
G Force (IRE) - 3yo
Gatewood (GB) - 4yo
Golden Horn (GB) - 3yo
Gutaifan (IRE) - 2yo
Hallowed Crown (AUS) - 3yo
Hillstar (GB) - 4yo
Hunter's Light (IRE) - 7yo
Karakontie (JPN) - 2yo

Kingston Hill (GB) - 3yo
Lucky Speed (IRE) - 3yo
Make Believe (GB) - 3yo
Muhaarar (GB) - 2yo, 3yo
Music Master (GB) - 4yo
Mustajeeb (GB) - 3yo
Night Of Thunder (IRE) - 4yo
Nutan (IRE) - 3yo
Prince Gibraltar (FR) - 4yo
Red Dubawi (IRE) - 6yo
Shooting To Win (AUS) - 3yo
Sidestep (AUS) - 2yo
The Wow Signal (IRE) - 2yo

Good-to-yielding
Cappella Sansevero (GB) - 2yo
Gleneagles (IRE) - 3yo
Mustajeeb (GB) - 4yo

Good-to-soft
Amaron (GB) - 3yo, 5yo, 6yo
Cable Bay (IRE) - 4yo
French Navy (GB) - 2yo, 3yo
Fulbright (GB) - 3yo
Hot Streak (IRE) - 2yo
Karakontie (JPN) - 3yo
Kingston Hill (GB) - 2yo
Make Believe (GB) - 3yo
Muhaarar (GB) - 3yo
Outstrip (GB) - 2yo
Red Dubawi (IRE) - 7yo
Sidestep (AUS) - 3yo

Yielding
Golden Horn (GB) - 3yo

Yielding-to-soft
Mustajeeb (GB) - 3yo

BY GOING DESCRIPTION FOR GROUP WINS

Soft
Amaron (GB) - 3yo
Earl Of Tinsdal (GER) - 3yo, 4yo
Evasive's First (FR) - 2yo
Hillstar (GB) - 4yo
Hot Streak (IRE) - 3yo
Hunter's Light (IRE) - 4yo
Karakontie (JPN) - 2yo
Kingston Hill (GB) - 2yo
Pether's Moon (IRE) - 4yo
Prince Gibraltar (FR) - 3yo
Supplicant (GB) - 2yo

Very soft
Amaron (GB) - 4yo
Lucky Speed (IRE) - 3yo
Pether's Moon (IRE) - 4yo
The Wow Signal (IRE) - 2yo

Heavy
Earl Of Tinsdal (GER) - 5yo
Gatewood (GB) - 6yo
Hallowed Crown (AUS) - 2yo, 3yo
Hunter's Light (IRE) - 4yo
Prince Gibraltar (FR) - 2yo

TAPETA
Standard
Hunter's Light (IRE) - 5yo

DIRT
Fast
American Pharoah (USA) - 2yo, 3yo

Sloppy
American Pharoah (USA) - 3yo

FRESHMAN SIRES OF 2019
BY CURRENT STUD FEE
(for those standing in the northern hemisphere)

Euros

€30,000 – Gleneagles (IRE)

€12,500 – Free Eagle (IRE)

€12,000 – Make Believe (GB)

€10,000 – Gutaifan (IRE)

€5,000 – Anjaal (GB)
€5,000 – Ivawood (IRE)
€5,000 – Kingston Hill (GB)

€4,500 – Amaron (GB)

€4,000 – Cappella Sansevero (GB)
€4,000 – Earl Of Tinsdal (GER)
€4,000 – French Navy (GB)
€4,000 – Fulbright (GB)
€4,000 – Hunter's Light (IRE)

€3,000 – Amarillo (IRE)
€3,000 – Galiway (GB)
€3,000 – Nutan (IRE)
€3,000 – Prince Gibraltar (FR)
€3,000 – Supplicant (GB)

€2,000 – Gatewood (GB)
€2,000 – Mustajeeb (GB)

€1,700 – Red Dubawi (IRE)

€1,500 – Lucky Speed (IRE)

on application – Hillstar (IRE)

Pounds
£50,000 – Golden Horn (GB)

£30,000 – Muhaarar (GB)

£15,000 – Night Of Thunder (IRE)

£7,000 – Brazen Beau (AUS)
£7,000 – Hot Streak (IRE)

£6,500 – Cable Bay (IRE)

£5,000 – Outstrip (GB)

£4,500 – Fountain Of Youth (IRE)

£4,000 – Due Diligence (USA)

£3,000 – Telescope (GB)

£1,750 – Intrinsic (GB)

private – Pether's Moon (IRE)

US Dollars
$110,000 – American Pharoah (USA)

$10,000 – Karakontie (JPN)

INDEX
(flat Group/Grade 1 winners and sires mentioned, including broodmare sires of the sales yearlings)

242

Major Emblem, 58
Make Believe, 150-6, 210, 213, 216-7, 220, 224, 228-9, 231-2, 235,
        238, 240
Makfi, 36, 57, 122-3, 150-1, 171-2, 184, 193, 199, 216-7, 220, 224
Malibu Moon, 10, 15, 30
Mamool, 6
Manduro, 2, 81, 101, 105, 107, 125, 175-6, 182, 191
Manila, 182
Marchand De Sable, 56
Maria's Mon, 14, 20, 39, 70
Marju, 29, 31, 44, 67, 105, 110-1, 119, 197
Mark Of Esteem, 20-1, 72, 95, 111, 114-5, 153, 173-4, 197, 224
Markaz, 99
Marooned, 42
Marquetry, 12
Marvellous, 85
Masar, 168
Master Carpenter, 144
Mastercraftsman, 44, 102, 115, 137, 143-4, 168, 191, 216-7, 220,
        224
Mastery, 33
Mayson, 34, 127
Meadowlake, 140
Meandre, 53
Mecca's Angel, 98
Medaglia d'Oro, 13, 22
Medicean, 22, 30-1, 44, 60, 63, 95, 104, 107, 135, 152, 154, 183,
        200
Menifee, 176
Midnight Storm, 10
Miesque, 137-8
Military Plume, 195-6
Mill Reef, 42, 148, 157, 180
Mind Games, 48, 50, 166
Miner's Mark, 182
Mineshaft, 13-4, 50, 137
Minstrella, 171-2
Mister Baileys, 204
Miswaki, 54, 81, 84, 87, 96, 168, 206
Mizzen Mast, 31, 77, 112

Printed in Poland
by Amazon Fulfillment
Poland Sp. z o.o., Wrocław